vuli and other plays

Kivuli

and other plays

Asiedu Yirenkyi

ONDON

HEINEMANN

BADAN · NAIROBI

Heinemann Educational Books Ltd
22 Bedford Square, London WC1B 3HH
P.M.B. 5205 Ibadan · P.O. Box 45314 Nairobi

EDINBURGH MELBOURNE AUCKLAND
HONG KONG SINGAPORE KUALA LUMPUR NEW DELHI
KINGSTON PORT OF SPAIN

Heinemann Educational Books Inc.
4 Front Sreet, Exeter, New Hampshire 03833, USA

ISBN 0 435 90216 4

Set, printed and bound in Great Britain by
Fakenham Press Limited,
Fakenham, Norfolk

Contents

To AFUA B–P

Kivuli

A Play in Three Acts

Kivuli was first performed by the Studio Players at the University of Ghana Drama Studio on 28, 29 February and 1, 2, 3, and 4 March 1972, with the following cast

KUMI MENSAH, *Ebow Erskine*
AUNTIE COMFORT, *Akosua Amo-Dako*
YAA ASI, *Marilyn Meyer*
APPEAH KUMI, *Owusu Prempeh*
MR ADOM, *Emmanuel Ayansu*
MR BLANKSON, *Ebow Daniel*
KWADWO OKOTO, *William Addo*
KWASI TWUM, *Yaw Okai*
AWO, *Mrs Patience Akunor*
THE MAN, *Anthony Kwesi*
SET DESIGNER, *Mrs Uwa Hunwick*

Directed by ASIEDU YIRENKYI

Characters
KUMI MENSAH, *Family head*
AUNTIE COMFORT, *Kumi Mensah's wife*
YAA ASI, *Kumi Mensah's daughter*
APPEAH KUMI, *Kumi Mensah's first male child and Yaa Asi's brother*
MR ADOM, *A village headteacher*
MR BLANKSON, LL.B. *A lawyer. Alias Samuel, William, Sebastian*
KWADWO OKOTO, *A parasite*
KWASI TWUM, *Grandson of Kumi Mensah*
AWO, *Kwadwo Okoto's mother*
AUNTIE AYELE, *Not a member of the family*

Scene: *A small farming village community*
Set: *Family head's house*

Notes from the playwright

A few points, as follow, may interest readers and producers.

1. Most of the off-stage dramatic actions in *Kivuli*, such as eavesdropping, Kumi's suicide, and Comfort's reaction to the chained dog, are all part of on-the-stage action. The set design should therefore be made to emphasize an image of a house with part of the backstage and compound revealed to the audience.

2. *Kivuali* may be performed on a proscenium stage and in an open-air theatre with little modification.

3. The traditional rituals of chiefs or elders speaking through intermediaries and some ritual praise poetry may be edited in productions but judgement here should be exercised so as not to sacrifice the character of Kumi Mensah.

The above comments should in no way prevent a producer from making his own creative decisions.

The Mind of Africa

It used to be commonly said in Africa that the eyes of the whole world were upon us.

The effect of this on action was that it depleted it of sincerity and balance. The eyes of the whole world are not on Africa.

If the eyes of Africa could be turned inwards, however, and bootless comparisons with other continents indulged in less, the African miracle might take place.

The independence of Africa will not amount to much unless Africa can be egocentric in action and self-image.

W. E. Abraham

Wo de w'aniwa abien hwe toa mu a wo hwene ntam na ehu mu.

An Akan proverb

ACT ONE

Set: A compound house. There are two doors upstage. Left door leads into the children's room. Right door leads into KUMI MENSAH's *room. Centre stage between the two doors is a large sitting room.*

The sitting room is sparsely furnished. There are a few old stools and chairs. There are two long benches upstage left and right; and centre stage is a smaller wicker table, overturned, from the previous night's quarrel.

Leading further downstage, on both left and right, are two fences with a gate in each. Left gate leads into the bathroom and into the kitchen. Right gate leads to the outside of the house and into the town.

The usual genuine village environment; birds singing, cocks crowing, ducks quacking and a dog barking. Slow light fade up.

Pause. KUMI MENSAH *enters from his bedroom. He is a dignified-looking man in his late fifties. He has handsome features and a youthful appearance. He wears a small piece of cloth tied on from the waist down.*

KUMI MENSAH: [*Searching*] Yaa . . . Yaa Asi!

Sees his towel carelessly thrown on his family stool, stage left. He picks up towel from stool. Pause, as KUMI MENSAH *looks at stool. Exits into bathroom.*

Enter YAA ASI *from bedroom. Yawns. Crosses slowly into kitchen. Re-enters, carelessly, holding a broom.* YAA ASI *is a girl of about 15, pretty and innocent-looking. She walks drowsily across stage. Sits. Gets up and begins calmly arranging the room. She stops; throws broom away and sits sluggishly with her hand supporting her jaw. She is lonely. Re-enter* KUMI MENSAH *from bathroom.*

KUMI MENSAH: [*Stops short. Shocked*] Yaa! Don't sit with your jaw propped in your hand like that! It's taboo!

YAA ASI: [*Straightens up. Blank face*]

KUMI MENSAH: What's wrong with you?

YAA ASI: [*Stands*] Nothing.

KUMI MENSAH: Hurry up and clean the house then! The lawyer is coming here this morning, you know that?

YAA ASI: Yes, Papa . . . [*She picks up the broom. Forgets herself as she stands gazing blankly*]

KUMI MENSAH: What are you waiting for? [*Pause*] Well . . . ? [*Pause: moves closer to* YAA ASI. YAA ASI *drops the broom*] What is wrong with you, Yaa?

YAA ASI: [*Rebellious*] Nothing. [*Long pause*]

KUMI MENSAH: You sure you're alright? [YAA ASI *does not answer. After a short pause*] Yes; I know what's wrong . . . Look at me. I know you're still sulky about yesterday. Patience; patience . . . I know Auntie Comfort sometimes demands too much of you. But have patience with her; do whatever she demands of you. You can complain to me about it later. You understand?

YAA ASI: I understand.

KUMI MENSAH: When your mother died, I was left all alone until Comfort came into my life. I can't do without her. Besides, I am your father; I can't be expected to take your side against my wife . . .

YAA ASI: [*Sharp*] I know.

KUMI MENSAH: Don't misunderstand me. You are my only daughter. I know that. But Comfort is my wife.

YAA ASI: I understand . . .

KUMI MENSAH: [*Relieved*] Good girl. Finish up with your cleaning. You have a few more errands to do for me this morning. [*He crosses to bedroom door*] I almost forgot. Did I tell you your brother is coming home on vacation this morning?

YAA ASI: I got his letter, yesterday.

KUMI MENSAH: I got one from him too. I hope your brother is reading his books well. I'm told . . . never mind; finish with your cleaning . . . [*Exits into his bedroom*]

YAA ASI: I'm told; they say; always some report about other people . . . Hmm . . . this Comfort . . . only the devil knows what . . . [*A dog barks and yelps backstage. Sudden anger*] And that dog too! Yelp! Yelp! Yelp! What is it you want? Are you chained up to this house? I even . . .

Re-enter KUMI MENSAH *with a bucket.*

KUMI MENSAH. What is it again, Yaa?

YAA ASI. I . . . I'm . . .

KUMI MENSAH: Never mind . . . Here; your mother wants you to prepare her some water for her bath. [*Gives her the bucket*] And hurry about the cleaning. The lawyer is arriving any minute! [*Exits*]

YAA ASI: Be patient! Clean the house! Fetch water for Comfort! [*She throws away the bucket*] She can fetch her own water! I'm tired, tired of them all!

Dog keeps barking. A moment later YAA ASI *picks the broom and continues the cleaning. Her back is turned to the gate leading outside. The gate opens. Enter* APPEAH KUMI. APPEAH *is about 17. He is dragging behind him a big portmanteau. He sets down the portmanteau without attracting attention, then tiptoes stealthily to his sister and . . .*

APPEAH: [*Tickling his sister's midriff*] Kwwww . . .

YAA ASI: [*Jumps up in fright*] Who's . . . Oh, it's you.

APPEAH: Of course it's me. Who else . . .

YAA ASI: You're here early. [*Picks up broom*]

APPEAH: Couldn't wait to . . .

YAA ASI: [*Turns away from* APPEAH *coldly*] Welcome home.

APPEAH: [*Surprised*] Hey . . . what's wrong?

YAA ASI: [*Cleaning*] I have not finished the cleaning.

APPEAH [*Grabs at the broom*] The cleaning can wait!

YAA ASI: Ohh . . . Appeah . . .

APPEAH: But why? Aren't you happy I'm home?

YAA ASI: Leave the broom!

APPEAH: Give me that!

YAA ASI: I've got to finish the cleaning . . .

Tug-of-war.

APPEAH: I've been away a whole year; you know that?

YAA ASI: [*Forcefully; almost pushes* APPEAH *down*] Let go!

APPEAH: What? Why this?

YAA ASI: [*Suddenly*] Tell me! Did you pass your promotion examination?

APPEAH: Of course I passed it.

YAA ASI: [*Sigh of relief*] Thank God.

APPEAH: Thank who?

YAA ASI: You passed your exam! The devil is shamed!

APPEAH: What the devil are you talking about?

YAA ASI: Shh . . . Stop shouting. Auntie Comfort is sleeping.

APPEAH: At this time? Sleeping at this time of day?

YAA ASI: You should know.

APPEAH: Hey, is that woman still up to her devilment?

YAA ASI: Things are worse now, Appeah.

APPEAH: Not on me! Because if that witch thinks she's got me for her
    slave again, then she'd better be prepared for some nastiness from
    me. I'm not going to take any more orders or nonsense from anybody,
    anywhere, at anytime and . . .

YAA ASI: Your temper, Appeah. It will not help you change anything in
    this house. [*Spies around*] That woman is practically leading Father by
    the nose now; and I bet you, the old man is going to do anything in
    the world just to gratify her. [*Confides*] Only yesterday, it was only
    yesterday, during a quarrel that I finally realized that it was she who
    asked Father to stop me from school.

APPEAH: Her reason?

YAA ASI: [*Fancy*] She needs somebody to help her with the house work.
    [*Picks up broom*] Well . . . maybe I don't count. But you . . . it is you
    I'm worried about.

APPEAH: You mean she could ask Father to stop me from school?

YAA ASI: Is that too much of a problem for her?

APPEAH: Please . . . [*Laughs*] Is that what's been bothering you? No . . . No . . . Please . . . [*laughs*] How?

YAA ASI: Don't laugh. I'm serious.

APPEAH: How can father stop me from school? I'm the top boy in my class, you know that?

YAA ASI: I was the top girl in my class too . . .

APPEAH: Please; stop worrying about the impossible. Her witchcraft . . .

YAA ASI: Shhhh . . .

APPEAH: [*Jumps up*] What is it?

YAA ASI: Shhhhh . . . [*Tiptoes to* KUMI MENSAH's *door*] A strange pair of ears . . .

APPEAH: Eavesdropper?

YAA ASI: [*Crossing back*] Don't ask me . . .

APPEAH: Somebody is trying to beat us at our own game, eh?

Brother and sister look at each other. They both burst into hilarious laughter. For a moment, they look like two very happy children.

YAA ASI: Ohh . . . Appeah, I'm so happy you're home. I'm sure things will work well now you're back. Go . . . go in . . . go in now. Go in and change up. I'll finish with the cleaning in a moment. Oh, Appeah, there's a lot to talk about later.

APPEAH: [*Grabs his portmanteau*] You bet there is.

YAA ASI: You leave the bag there. I will carry it in for you.

APPEAH: It's too heavy for you.

YAA ASI: I can handle it. Watch me! I'm going to bet you I can lift it with my one finger.

APPEAH: You can?

YAA ASI: Easily. [*Attempts lifting the bag*] UUUUhhhhh . . . Why? This thing is very heavy! What do you have in there? Stones or what?

APPEAH: Books! A few clothes, that's all.

YAA ASI: [*Suddenly*] You remind me! Did you bring back the cloth? I mean the 'Kente' cloth you borrowed from Father for your speech day?

APPEAH: Has she been talking about that too?

YAA ASI: But you should know!

APPEAH: [*Impassioned*] I thought: I am my father's eldest son and the next in line for his possessions. Why should anybody break her neck over my wearing one 'Kente' cloth which, come to it, is mine.

YAA ASI: Are you sure of what you're saying? That you have a right to Father's property?

APPEAH: Who else should inherit his father's property but the eldest male child?

YAA ASI: Have you ever wondered why Auntie Comfort hates us?

APPEAH: She's a devil, that's all.

YAA ASI: That's what you think. I think it's all because of her son, Kwasi.

APPEAH: Kwasi? How does he come into this?

YAA ASI: [*In a whisper*] You see; if you are out of the way, Kwasi comes first in line of succession. That's all the reason. Auntie Comfort wants you out of the way of her son. And Father? Well . . . I don't blame him. An old man of sixty blessed with a fresh woman of twenty-five. What resistance can you expect from him?

APPEAH: And who's been feeding you with all this?

YAA ASI: I haven't been eavesdropping every day for nothing.

APPEAH: Well . . . I must say I'm surprised. Really surprised. The whole thing sounds silly. That woman must be mad. Who cares about family property? I want to help myself; be dependent on myself . . . that's why I'm still in school. I want to be a master of my own house. Who cares about a bunch of illiterates sitting up all year round waiting for somebody to die so they can begin fighting over property? It's all silly. Silly and backward. Let's talk about something else. [*Crosses to portmanteau*]

YAA ASI: Well . . .

APPEAH: I'm hungry. Any food in the house?

YAA ASI: You go in and change up. I'll have to heat up the stew. [APPEAH *picks up portmanteau. Crosses to his bedroom door*] Leave the bag there. I'm carrying it inside for you.

APPEAH: Never mind. I'll carry it in myself.

Enter KUMI MENSAH. *He is well dressed in a rich new cloth.*

KUMI MENSAH: [*To* APPEAH] Oh, you're here already.

APPEAH: Yes, Father.

KUMI MENSAH: You're early.

Long pause. Father and son look at each other.

KUMI MENSAH: [*Embarrassed*] I received your school report today . . . no . . . yesterday. [*Pause*] You performed well. [*Wry smile*]

APPEAH: Thank you.

KUMI MENSAH: Oh . . . Yaa . . . ehhh . . . ; here is a list. Go to the market and buy a turkey . . . fat one; some eggs; schnapps and . . . you have everything written there. Here is some money. [KUMI MENSAH *turns to exit, stumbles over the family stool. Anger*] And get that stool out of here! [*Exits*]

APPEAH: [*Calmly sits on his portmanteau*] What do you want a turkey and schnapps and all that for?

YAA ASI: [*Picks up stool*] Celebration.

APPEAH: What celebration?

YAA ASI: [*Places stool against* KUMI MENSAH'S *bedroom door*] Celebrating the first day a lawyer is coming to this village.

APPEAH: What lawyer?

YAA ASI: You know, the lawyer representing him on that land case. He is coming here this morning. An enlightened London-trained lawyer is visiting some poor village dwellers; we must impress him, showering him with presents.

APPEAH: Just what is wrong with that old man? Can't he outlive the past? Five years wrangling over a piece of land; and all to whose benefit? If your brother made his cocoa farm on somebody's land and he is dead, and the land-owner is claiming back his own land, whatever is there to fight about?

YAA ASI: I don't know, Appeah. Most of the time I don't understand Father myself. It seems his whole purpose in life is to please the whole wide world but his own children. Let any stranger die anywhere miles around the village; and that sets it all up. He will begin deducing and deducting from some dead family lineage, and eventually end up fitting the dead person some place in a family relation you can never understand. And that justifies wasting weeks at funerals. Before it's all over, what was saved from the lawyer is squandered at a funeral.

APPEAH: Waste! Waste! All that money could have paid for your secondary education; but does he think about his own children's future? No! Work! Work! You work to death on his cocoa farm; while he spends the money on some ungrateful blood-sucking parasites!

YAA ASI: You and your big English.

APPEAH: Who's his brother's keeper today anyway? The fashion today is: hit on some loot; get all you want for yourself and, why, the rest of the world can also take care of itself. So lawyer's fee or no lawyer's fee, funerals or no funerals . . .

YAA ASI: Quiet!

APPEAH: Who is it?

YAA ASI: Shhhhhhhh . . .

APPEAH: Who?

YAA ASI: Shhhhh . . . She's coming!

APPEAH: I'm going . . .

APPEAH *rushes for his portmanteau;* YAA ASI *picks up the bucket. The door to* KUMI MENSAH'S *room opens slowly.* AUNTIE COMFORT *strolls majestically into the sitting room. Comfort is about twenty-five; a very pretty woman. She is a little over-dressed for the morning.*

COMFORT: Hey Appeah! Come here! Come here! And you too, Yaa Asi, don't run away! Come over here! [YAA ASI *and* APPEAH *on one side, confront* COMFORT] Don't your schools these days teach you a little bit about respect? [*Silence*] That's what I mean. No respect. Not a little bit of respect! Three years, only three years. Just three years in a secondary school and look at it . . . you think you are ten foot tall! Go your way! Go! Don't waste your precious time talking to a body like me. [APPEAH *exits, dragging his portmanteau with him*] [*Shouts to* APPEAH] And you better take off that white shirt and clean trousers. We wear rags here but we work hard. That's how we get your school fees paid! [*Pause*] [*To* YAA ASI] Is the water ready?

YAA ASI: Please, Auntie . . . I was . . .

COMFORT: You didn't fetch it. I know you won't fetch it! After all, who is that 'lady' called Comfort that the 'princess' Yaa Asi should fetch water for her?

YAA ASI: Please, Auntie . . .

COMFORT: [*Attempts to snatch the bucket from* YAA ASI] Give me that bucket! I'm not lazy like you.

YAA ASI: Auntie, please; it's not that I didn't want to . . . I . . . was cleaning the room and . . .

COMFORT: Lies! Lies and excuses. Always lies and flimsy excuses. [COMFORT *shouts to attract her husband's attention*] I asked you to fetch me a bucket of water . . . only one bucket of water. But of course, your breasts are almost as round as mine . . . so who serves who? [*Enter* KUMI MENSAH. COMFORT *pretends she has not seen him. Calculated coolness*] You think I didn't hear you and that lazy brother of yours shouting and carousing all over the house. Don't tell me you were cleaning this house. [*Snatches bucket violently*] Give me that bucket! I'll fetch the water myself.

KUMI MENSAH: [*Commanding*] Yaa Asi, take the bucket back from your mother!

COMFORT: Oh, don't bother her. I'll fetch the water myself.

KUMI MENSAH: No! Let her do that! She will do it! [*He takes the bucket from* COMFORT *and places it centre of stage*] Pick it up! I say pick it up! NOW! How long is it since I gave you that bucket? [*Pause*] [YAA ASI *is almost in tears. He threatens her with his sandals*] I said pick up that bucket! You hear me! [YAA ASI *quickly picks the bucket up. Exits now in tears*] And next time you better do what you are asked to do. And quick! I don't encourage delinquency in this house.

COMFORT: [*Begins dusting the room*] Look . . . look at all this. A living room that now looks like a dunghill. This is what our 'princess' says she's spent a whole morning cleaning.

KUMI MENSAH: Leave the dusting. She is coming . . .

COMFORT: Let me clean it. [*Dusting*] When I see so much dust around, my stomach simply churns.

KUMI MENSAH: [*Henpecked*] Let me give you a hand then. [*The two dusting*] The lawyer will soon be here. Everything here must look clean and impressive.

COMFORT: [*Sits*] You remind me. Have you sent for the presents?

KUMI MENSAH: I gave the money to Yaa Asi. I don't know what's getting into that girl recently!

COMFORT: I was thinking . . . Don't you think a bottle of whisky and a bottle of schnapps can be equally impressive?

Enter YAA ASI.

YAA ASI: [*To* COMFORT] The water is ready, Auntie.

KUMI MENSAH: Yaa.

YAA ASI: Yes, Father.

KUMI MENSAH: Buy a bottle each of the drinks mentioned on the list there. And go right now! The lawyer is arriving any time.

YAA ASI: Yes, Father.

Exit YAA ASI.

KUMI MENSAH: Your water is ready.

COMFORT: [*Starts cleaning*] I'll tidy this place up a bit. [*Pause*]

KUMI MENSAH: Comfort.

COMFORT: Yes, K.

KUMI MENSAH: Do you still think we should hire a second lawyer? Like I said, my opponent was represented by three lawyers last week and for the first time, it looked like I'd lost the case already.

COMFORT: Kumi, if more lawyers are necessary to help win the case, then, I say, HIRE MORE LAWYERS! You must not allow this land to be taken away from the family. Land is not just property; IT IS LIFE. You are not engaged in a fight for a piece of land. You are fighting for the very survival of the family. You can't afford to lose this case.

KUMI MENSAH: But money! I'm being drained out . . . before this land dispute first came up, I could say with all confidence I was a man! Now I am almost . . . [*Pause*] Last year, I had to stop Yaa Asi from school. This year, Appeah's college fees . . . Well . . . I don't know . . .

COMFORT: But where is your problem, Kumi?

KUMI MENSAH: Don't you see . . . [*After a short pause*] If I didn't fight this case to the end, it will bring a big disgrace on me. I would have failed in my very important collective commitment to the family. On the other hand, my son's education is my personal commitment; if I ignore that, what is . . . the rest of the village going to say about me? I don't know what to do now . . .

COMFORT: Kumi, you don't want to compare the value of acquiring land to that of educating a child. My uncle used to say, 'Educate a child and you have provided a life-style for a single individual! Buy land and you have provided, permanently, for the whole generation of a family.' That's why my uncle stopped me from school. And I don't regret it. Why? Educated men die and get buried with all their knowledge; but the lands my great-great-grandfathers bought are still servicing the family. But, Appeah is not my son. I can't suggest anything about his future to his father.

KUMI MENSAH: Hmmm . . . well . . . Tomorrow's problem may bring its own solution.

Sound of a car stopping outside. Dog barking.

COMFORT: Did I hear a car pull up?

KUMI MENSAH: A car?

Banging of car door. Dog barking.

KUMI MENSAH: Yes. But . . . but . . . the road is hardly wide enough for a car.

COMFORT: I must change into something brighter. I feel so . . .

KUMI MENSAH: You look pretty enough . . .

COMFORT: Do I?

KUMI MENSAH: Here . . . give me a hand. Get the broom . . . and those rags too . .

COMFORT *and* KUMI MENSAH *run helter-skelter, putting things in order. A moment later, the gate to the right of the stage opens.* MR BLANKSON *in a well-timed, theatrical fashion, strides majestically in. He is a heavy-set, pot-bellied man in his late forties: heavily attired in a two-piece woollen* [*Western*] *suit. A felt hat on and umbrella for his walking stick. He carries also an expensive brief case and is smoking a fat cigar.*

KUMI MENSAH: You are exactly on time, Mr Lawyer.

MR BLANKSON: Time! Time! Time is money! [*Laughs loud*]

KUMI MENSAH: I'll take your bag, sir.

MR BLANKSON: Thank you. [*Puffs a thick plume of smoke*]

KUMI MENSAH: . . . And your hat.

MR BLANKSON: Thank you very much [*Produces a handkerchief*] Oh, rough! Rough and tough! Very tough!

KUMI MENSAH: I never thought one could drive through on a bush path.

MR BLANKSON: I ploughed through it alright! The new car I have back there . . . powerful. Powerful but very expensive! [*Laughs.* COMFORT *positions a chair*]

COMFORT: Sit down, Mr Lawyer.

MR BLANKSON: No . . . no . . . not yet. [*Grins*] I have not greeted you formally, you know. The custom . . . custom, they say 'makes or models manners of man'. [*Laughs loud*] Or you think because I come from the city, I have no respect for our sacred traditions. No . . . no. No, sir. No tradition, no Lawyer Blankson! [*Shakes hands with* KUMI MENSAH] How are you, old man?

KUMI MENSAH: The Gods are on my side.

MR BLANKSON: [*Looks seductively at* COMFORT. *Puffs from cigar*] Uuuuuhhhhh . . . and eh . . . this charming lady . . . She's the daughter of yours you were talking about the other day. Right?

KUMI MENSAH: That's my wife, Comfort.

MR BLANKSON: Oh, well . . . I see . . . [*Trying to be humorous*] Well, old man, I must say you have such perfect taste. Just perfect . . . [*Shakes hands with* COMFORT] How are you, Mrs Mensah?

COMFORT: [*Recites*] Pretty well; thank you.

MR BLANKSON: Frankly, Mr Mensah; I nearly . . . well, I thought she was your daughter. I was going to say, 'How on earth didn't I come to this house before!' [*Laughs loud*] Oh yes; I am not joking. Not at all. You provincials have a monopoly on true beauty.
[*Pointing and almost touching* COMFORT] Just you look at such a perfect woman. A truly faultless figure of a perfect woman. Perfect with no paints; no ponds and no simulations! That's beauty truly blended!

COMFORT: [*Flattered*] Oh . . . Mr Lawyer.

MR BLANKSON: I mean it. I really do. You know, the kind of women one sees around the cities these days. One can't tell whether the face is painted or scaled or sprayed! And the skirt? Right this high. Disgusting! That's the trouble; one can't find . . .

KUMI MENSAH: Won't you sit down, sir?

MR BLANKSON: Oh . . . Thank you. Thank you. [*Sits*] Thank you very much. Well . . . well . . . sometimes, I just keep running on . . . like . . . like a tap! [*Laugh loudly*]

KUMI MENSAH: [*Calling*] Appeah! Appeah!

VOICE: Yes, Father.

KUMI MENSAH: Bring the lawyer some good drinking water.

MR BLANKSON: [*Sneezes*] Oh . . . terrible! Just suffocating! Wish I could take my coat off . . .

KUMI MENSAH: Comfort, help the lawyer with his coat.

COMFORT: Let me help you with your coat, sir.

MR BLANKSON: No, no, no. I can't take off my coat. I mustn't.

BLANKSON *puffs thick cigar smoke.* KUMI MENSAH *and* COMFORT *are uncomfortable. Enter* APPEAH *with the water.*

KUMI MENSAH: Appeah, you shouldn't have used the mug! Where's my drinking glass?

MR BLANKSON: It's alright, Mr Mensah. I love drinking from a mug! In fact, a calabash would have made me feel even more at home.
[*Gets up and pours libation*] Here's to you, our great ancestral spirits. Make us rich and powerful! [*Sips some water*] [*Points*] This is your son. No mistake this time!

KUMI MENSAH: Yes. My eldest son by my late wife. I have another boy who's about four . . .

MR BLANKSON: Your wife died?

KUMI MENSAH: Yes, my first wife. About eight years ago.

MR BLANKSON: What a pity! What a pity! My mother died too when I was about seven years old. And my old man married another woman. She was a lazy woman. And, boy, it was the hardest time in my life. But I managed to pull through it alright. Patience! Patience pays they say. [*Laughs*]

KUMI MENSAH: You are educated people; our traditional life shouldn't mean anything to you.

MR BLANKSON: I do envy our traditional life, you know. I really do. You don't know how lucky you provincials are. Look at me, for example, I have to wake myself up every morning at eight on thick black coffee. Poison! Just plain black poison! But what can I do; if you don't drink coffee, they say, you are not civilized. Oh . . . I'm running on again. I'm such a talkative . . . [*Handing over the mug*] You are in a secondary school, am I right?

APPEAH: Yes, sir.

MR BLANKSON: Which secondary school?

APPEAH: Benkum, sir.

MR BLANKSON: [*Strong accent*] Benkum? That's a very good school. A very good school! What form are you in?

APPEAH: Form Four, sir.

MR BLANKSON: Very encouraging. Very! [*Pause*] Look carefully at me.

APPEAH: Yes, sir.

MR BLANKSON: Do you like my suit?

APPEAH: Yes, sir.

MR BLANKSON: [*Turns out coat lining*] Would you like to see yourself wearing something like this some day?

APPEAH: Yes, sir.

MR BLANKSON: Then you must study hard in school. These days paper qualifications are the easiest way to a comfortable life.

APPEAH: Yes, sir.

MR BLANKSON: You may go now. And thank you for the wonderful water.

APPEAH: Yes, sir. [*Exit* APPEAH]

MR BLANKSON: That's a boy! That's a boy! Wonderful! Cultured! Very cultured! I like him. I really do. Did you notice the way he answered my questions? In very simple and humble 'Yes, sirs.' That's what I mean by 'cultured boy'. Mr Mensah, I'll encourage you on this. Save all you can and send that boy to London for further studies. They say, 'LEARN A LITTLE LAW IN LONDON AND BE TWICE AS WISE AS THE SERPENT.' [*Laughs loudly*]

KUMI MENSAH: I'm doing my best for him, Mr Lawyer. [*To* COMFORT] Let's welcome our visitor. [*To lawyer*] It's our turn to welcome you formally here, Mr Lawyer.

MR BLANKSON: Well . . . We were carried away by the conversation, weren't we? All my fault. It's all my fault. Sometimes I'm such a talkative . . . [*Laughs*]

KUMI MENSAH: [*Shakes hands with lawyer*] Welcome to our humble home, Mr Lawyer.

MR BLANKSON: Thank you.

COMFORT: [*Shakes hands*; MR BLANKSON *takes a firm grip on her*] I welcome you, Mr Lawyer.

MR BLANKSON: Blankson. Mr Blankson. Samuel William Sebastian Blankson! Here! My card!

COMFORT: For me?

MR BLANKSON: Yes, for you.

KUMI MENSAH: Comfort . . .

COMFORT: Yes.

KUMI MENSAH: You'll have to stand in as my interpreter.

COMFORT: I'll try . . .

KUMI MENSAH: Well, then. Let Mr Lawyer . . .

MR BLANKSON: Mr Blankson.

KUMI MENSAH: Let Mr Blankson know that we are all well here and feeling fine . . .

COMFORT: That's what my husband says. 'We are all well and feeling fine.' [MR BLANKSON *looks at his watch*]

MR BLANKSON: God!

KUMI MENSAH: It is he who has travelled.

COMFORT: My husband says 'It is you who have travelled.' [MR BLANKSON *clears his throat; looks at his watch*]

MR BLANKSON: Hot! Hot around here . . .

KUMI MENSAH: [*Unperturbed by the lawyer's uneasiness*] And travellers have . . .

MR BLANKSON: Well . . . eh . . . I don't mean, Mr Mensah, to cut you off like that but . . . time; time is money! [*Laughs*] Let's to business.

KUMI MENSAH: That's what I was coming to next.

MR BLANKSON: [*Takes on the strictly businessman's attitude*] Well . . . oh where do we start? Where do we start . . . I got it! Got it! You know, my mind sometimes slips off . . . Much unlike a good lawyer. I need a tranquillizer. [*Lights a new cigar*] Mind?

KUMI MENSAH: No.

MR BLANKSON: Wonderful. [*Puffs cigar*] Well . . . eh . . . I . . . promised to call here personally today . . . to discuss the new turn of the case . . . and to think with you about the possibility of hiring a second lawyer. Right?

KUMI MENSAH: Right.

MR BLANKSON: [*Pause. Puffs at cigar*] Ashtray?

COMFORT: Leave the ash on the floor.

MR BLANKSON: Charming. Charming of you.

COMFORT: No mention, Mr Lawyer.

MR BLANKSON: [*After a few seconds*] Ehhhh . . . where was I? Yes . . . yes . . . I know. I got it! [*Laughs*] I've gone through the whole case carefully. And . . . [*Pause*] . . . let me put it this way. Things are going against us. That's the hard fact. Or to put it in other words, we are going to lose this case if we don't act fast! You see, this case has some special . . . inherent twists and turns and complications . . .

KUMI MENSAH: Complications? I thought my case was simple. You said so yourself some time ago.

MR BLANKSON: Don't misunderstand me. It's the facts . . . the facts of the case are simple. But courts don't operate on facts. In court, one wins or loses a case on substance and technicalities. It is like a game and the tactic of the game is the essence of the game; facts are second fiddle in law. We have, therefore, to base our case on the tactic and technicalities that could in fact, be the facts of the case.

KUMI MENSAH: It sounds more and more confusing . . .

MR BLANKSON: To the layman, yes! But let the lawyers worry about that. Now, to the facts. Your brother . . . elder brother . . . leased this land right?

KUMI MENSAH: Right.

MR BLANKSON: And in the tenancy agreement was it stipulated that YOUR BROTHER should work on the farm and he – mind you, he, not you – he and the landowner share the profits or the proceeds; right?

KUMI MENSAH: I'm listening . . .

MR BLANKSON: See the complication I'm driving at?

KUMI MENSAH: Well . . . I don't know anything about law . . .

MR BLANKSON: I'll explain it in layman's language. Your brother didn't buy the land. Agreed?

KUMI MENSAH: Yes.

MR BLANKSON: So according to law, he has no title to the land. Understand me so far?

KUMI MENSAH: Yes.

MR BLANKSON: Then in the tenancy agreement, only your brother . . . your brother only was mentioned . . . by his name.

KUMI MENSAH: Right.

MR BLANKSON: [Overpleased about his progress. Puffs at cigar] Does it sound like everything is lost already?

KUMI MENSAH: Well . . . I don't know law . . .

MR BLANKSON: [Laughs loudly] Don't lose hope, old man. We have a strong case! Very strong case! We only have to convince the court that YOU, the chosen successor to your brother, are the same as your brother. And have the right to the farm just as your brother had! That is our case!

COMFORT: I don't know anything about law . . . but do you think we will win a case like this?

MR BLANKSON: Mrs Mensah: a lawyer is like a boxer; always fight and win it! Like they say in law schools: 'Never give up a fight until you are knocked down dead.'

KUMI MENSAH: I'll never give up this land too! Man is made to fight! The landowner thinks I have no mettle in me! We shall see! We shall drag this case on; in and out of every court. High court if that is what it calls for . . .

MR BLANKSON: [*Flicking ash off cigar*] I fully understand your feelings, Mr Mensah. [*Flicks ash off cigar*] I'm going to leave your house all in ashes.

COMFORT: Don't trouble.

MR BLANKSON: Well then. Let's to the centre of all central problems. Money! [*Laughs loudly*]

KUMI MENSAH: How much do you think . . . eh . . .

MR BLANKSON: [*Polite grin*] Don't be frightened of me, old man.

KUMI MENSAH: Well . . . eh . . . just that things are harder this season . . .

MR BLANKSON: It won't be too hard for you. I know it won't be difficult on you men of the land . . . But let's get on to a little more honest talk! Shall we?

KUMI MENSAH: Yes, sir.

MR BLANKSON: Lawyers are by nature greedy. But . . . eh . . . let's say I'm the honest type . . . or better still a good friend. That puts me in the position of being both your friend, your adviser and your lawyer. Agreed?

KUMI MENSAH: I'm listening.

MR BLANKSON: Good. Now, as your adviser and a friend, allow me to . . . let me put it this way. I think you've spent too much money on this case. If you still want to go on with it you're certainly going to spend even more. The point I'm trying to make is that the market fluctuates and cocoa trees don't live forever!

COMFORT: You're right . . . But . . . what our dead relatives left behind cannot be abandoned.

MR BLANKSON: Don't misunderstand me. I'm not saying you should give up the case. Not at all . . . not at all . . . I stand for justice for the defenceless. And nothing gives me more pleasure than to lead in a case like this. But, you know, in law terms, we have something called eh . . . professional cost. That must be fully met.

KUMI MENSAH: How much is that?

MR BLANKSON: Not much. Only [*Speaks as though one word*] one thousand.

COMFORT: Pounds or cedis?

MR BLANKSON: Cedis.

KUMI MENSAH: And your fee?

MR BLANKSON: Later. 'The later the better', they say. [*Grins*]

KUMI MENSAH: Let's now . . . [*In a deep mood*] I have to make plans for the payment.

MR BLANKSON: Well . . . if you . . . [*Flicks more ash*] I . . . I must say, we lawyers have such a sensitive nature; humanity is our soft spot. I really hate to pile debts on good people like . . .

KUMI MENSAH: You come to it. If it's too much, we shall beg for reduction.

MR BLANKSON: Well . . . I'll try to be moderate [*Flicks ash*] Let me make it eight hundred.

KUMI MENSAH: Cedis?

MR BLANKSON: Cedis.

COMFORT: That comes to one thousand eight hundred.

MR BLANKSON: You provincials are so divine in your calculations. Just divine!

KUMI MENSAH: Hmmm . . . one thousand eight hundred. Mr Blankson, I'll consult my wife for a moment.

MR BLANKSON: Time . . . time . . . is . . .

COMFORT: We won't be long. [*Exit* KUMI MENSAH *and* COMFORT]

MR BLANKSON: [*Stretches himself to shake off all the theatrics*] Ohhhhh . . . Hell! So hot . . . Africa is too hot!

MR BLANKSON *selects fresh cigar; lights it and begins puffing away. Pacing up and down, picks up a school report form on the table. Reads the report.* KUMI MENSAH *and* COMFORT *re-enter.*

MR BLANKSON: [*Defensively*] I was glancing through your son's school report. Very encouraging. Highly!

KUMI MENSAH: We didn't take too much of your time, I hope.

MR BLANKSON: No . . . no. Not at all; not at all!

KUMI MENSAH: Shall we sit down?

MR BLANKSON: Right. Right. Absolutely!

KUMI MENSAH: Well . . . we hit on a thousand, eight hundred . . .

MR BLANKSON: [*Sneezes*] Ahhh . . . excuse! The heat. Ohh . . . hot!

KUMI MENSAH: Well . . . Mr Blankson, I'll go right to the point.

MR BLANKSON: [*Applying his handkerchief*] Ha! This heat!

COMFORT: Your coat . . .

MR BLANKSON: The coat is fine. It's my tie; too tight! But go on . . . go on, Mr Mensah. I'm listening to you.

KUMI MENSAH: Well . . . Mr Blankson; this is the time of the year that proverbially we say, it rains alright but there is drought. You see, the cocoa season is almost ended and with my many other family responsibilities, I'll beg you to reduce the fee a bit.

MR BLANKSON: Heavens no! I'm afraid, Mr Mensah, lawyers don't bargain in their fees.

COMFORT: Bargaining is part of the fun of life. Besides . . .

MR BLANKSON: Okay . . . okay . . . ; I'll do a friend a favour. Only to you, mind! How much can you pay?

KUMI MENSAH: A thousand cedis.

MR BLANKSON: Too small. Come up a bit.

KUMI MENSAH: These are bad times. Next week, for example, I have to attend the third funeral celebration of my uncle's brother's wife. And that's not all; you never can tell when the next messenger is arriving with bad news. And I have to pull out money in all these troubles from my own pocket. I have practically nobody in the world to come to my aid.

COMFORT: Mr Blankson, we will give you a thousand two hundred.

MR BLANKSON: Come up small.

KUMI MENSAH: Thousand three hundred.

MR BLANKSON: Thousand three hundred and ninety-five.

COMFORT: That's fair enough.

KUMI MENSAH: [*Confused*] Well . . . eh . . . I . . . [*Pause*] [*With a little anger to* COMFORT] You have the money! What are you waiting for?

COMFORT: It's short of three hundred and ninety-five . . .

KUMI MENSAH: [*Desperately*] Give him what you have! Mr Blankson, we shall send the balance tomorrow! [COMFORT *unties her 'aboso' and produces bundles of currency notes*]

MR BLANKSON: [*At the same time*] Hww . . . the heat! Horrible! Africa is . . . [COMFORT *hands money to* MR BLANKSON]

MR BLANKSON: I trust you . . . absolutely! [*Packs money in brief case and locks it secure. Slaps brief case as he stands and stretches up. Looks at his watch*] Well; almost ten forty-five. I have to be in court by twelve. Time . . . Time is money! [*Smiles*]

KUMI MENSAH: I sent my daughter to the market to buy you a few presents . . .

MR BLANKSON: My time, Mr Mensah . . .

COMFORT: Yaa Asi too has kept too long . . .

KUMI MENSAH: I don't know what's got into that girl recently. She'll come and meet me . . .

MR BLANKSON: I really must be going . . .

KUMI MENSAH: I'm sorry my daughter is still not here with the presents. We will send them along tomorrow.

MR BLANKSON: Do that. [*Drops stub of cigar on the floor as he shakes hands with the couple. With left hand in half-salute*] Thank you very much, Mr Mensah. And Comfort, thanks for your wonderful service.

COMFORT: Bye, Mr Blankson.

KUMI MENSAH: I'll carry the bag to your car.

MR BLANKSON: Thank you. [*Crosses to gate*] Bye again, Comfort. [*Puts his hand on* KUMI MENSAH'S *shoulder as they both make for the exit*] Now that the money part is settled the lawyer's work begins . . . and you can count on me . . . [*Exit*]

COMFORT: [*Calls*] Appeah! Appeah! Appeah Kumi!

APPEAH: [*From the room*] Yes . . . Auntie.

COMFORT: What are you doing there in the room?

APPEAH: Nothing, Auntie.

COMFORT: Nothing? Hurry up and come out here! [*Pause*] Where are you?

APPEAH: I am coming!

APPEAH *enters sill in his white sthirt and tie.*

COMFORT: [*Utterly shocked*] Are you still in your white shirt and tie?
APPEAH: Auntie . . . I . . .
COMFORT: Look here, Appeah, we don't break our back here to pay your
way through college so you can come in here and teach us how to
dress up like . . . [*Mumbling to himself,* APPEAH *crosses into his room*]
Where are you going?
APPEAH: [*In anger*] I'm going to change my shirt. Why?
COMFORT: Don't you have a little manners to . . . [APPEAH *enters his
room banging the door*] Okay, go on . . . go on! Insult me in there! Go
on insulting me. Insult me in the room!
VOICE: Who's . . .
COMFORT: Oh . . . you can insult me. You don't bother me a bit!
[COMFORT *crosses to her bedroom door. Crosses back*] Hurry up and
change up all the same. You are going to the farm to bring some
food. You can insult me a billion times; you are going to the farm!
[*Crosses the stage*] We have to have food in the house, if you must eat!
[*Enter* YAA ASI] Oh . . . now, our princess Yaa is back.
YAA ASI: Yes, Auntie.
COMFORT: [*With irony*] You are a very good girl. Your father will be here
soon to congratulate you on your coming back so early.

Exit COMFORT *into the bathroom.* YAA ASI *puts down the shopping. Enter*
APPEAH *from room. He is very annoyed and cursing to himself.*

YAA ASI: Appeah . . .

APPEAH *does not answer.* YAA ASI *crosses into the kitchen. Enter* KUMI
MENSAH *from outside.*

KUMI MENSAH: Oh, Yaa, you're back now.
YAA ASI: Yes, Father . . .
KUMI MENSAH: The lawyer left. Never mind. Keep those things safe. I'm
sending Comfort to deliver them tomorrow.
YAA ASI: Yes, Father.

Enter APPEAH *with basket and holding a cutlass.*

KUMI MENSAH: Where are you going to, Appeah?
APPEAH: Farm.
KUMI MENSAH: Can you go alone?
APPEAH: I can.
KUMI MENSAH: It's not safe. I killed a python around the farm about a
month ago. Yaa . . . why don't you go with your brother and . . .
YAA ASI: Yes, Father. [YAA ASI *quickly takes the basket from* APPEAH]
COMFORT: [*Enters*] Yaa Asi, where are you going?

KUMI MENSAH: She's going to help Appeah on the farm. Do you want her to do something for you?

COMFORT: It's alright. The water, it's cold again but . . .

KUMI MENSAH: You two can go now. [*Exit* APPEAH *and* YAA ASI]

COMFORT: [*Crossing into her room*] Well . . . I need some soap.

KUMI MENSAH: Comfort . . . there's something . . .

COMFORT: Yes . . . what?

KUMI MENSAH: [*Haltingly*] You know . . . if we send this money to the lawyer . . . we will have practically nothing left in the safe. Appeah is on vacation . . .

COMFORT: You like to have problems, Kumi, that's why you keep having them. Just look at the huge sums of money you waste away paying school fees. And all to whose benefit? Who knows when one is going to die, anyway? If something happens to Appeah today, everything is wasted. I can't inherit his knowledge. Neither can you or anybody else in the family. So what's the use of sending the boy to school at all . . . except, of course, to provide for his selfish end? You may think I envy your children. Well . . . I have my own problems.

KUMI MENSAH: Hmm . . . maybe . . . tomorrow's problems will bring their own solution.

COMFORT: It's your headache. [*About to enter the room*] By the way, I must buy a few clothes for Kwasi. We haven't bought him any new clothes for over three months . . .

KUMI MENSAH: When are you bringing that boy back home? He's been with his grandparents too long.

COMFORT: They are not complaining.

KUMI MENSAH: That's not the point. You know there's hardly any money . . .

COMFORT: How much? How much, at all, can a boy of four spend . . .

KUMI MENSAH: Try to understand . . .

COMFORT: Don't send him any money! I'll send him money myself! [*Turns*]

KUMI MENSAH: Are you annoyed?

COMFORT: Don't touch me!

KUMI MENSAH: Listen here . . .

COMFORT: Leave me alone! I hate men who don't know their own children [*She dashes out of the room*]

KUMI MENSAH: Comfort . . . [*Rushes after her*]

Blackout. Baying of a wounded dog is heard from a distance.

END OF ACT ONE

ACT TWO

Set: Same as in Act One. Dawn: early birds are chirping; crickets whistling; guinea fowls squawking. A cock crows. Lights down to fading point. Enter KUMI MENSAH. *He sits lonely for a while. Lights his pipe. A moment passes. Cock crows. Enter* APPEAH KUMI. *He has a lantern. Lights up.*

APPEAH: You sent for me, Father?

KUMI MENSAH: Oh, you're here. Sit down.

APPEAH *sits, placing the lantern centre upstage, between himself and his father.*

KUMI MENSAH: [*Smokes for a while*] Ehhh . . . [*Clears his throat*] Ehhh . . . Appeah, did you bring all your things back home from school?

APPEAH: No, Father. [*Pause*] If you're talking about the 'Kente' cloth; yes, I have it with me.

KUMI MENSAH: Never mind. [*A long pause.* KUMI MENSAH *smokes for a while. Clears his throat*] Ehh . . . Appeah.

APPEAH: Yes, Father.

KUMI MENSAH: Do you know why our elders want to discuss very important family matters mostly at dawn?

APPEAH: No, Father.

KUMI MENSAH: Well . . . ehh . . . You see, man is said to be most sober at dawn. Again, it is said, a man who has no secrets has no soul. Walls have ears. I want to discuss something important with you but it is so important that you should keep it between the two of us ONLY. Nobody outside this house should ever know anything about it. You understand?

APPEAH: I understand.

KUMI MENSAH *smokes for a while.*

KUMI MENSAH: [*Puts away his pipe*] Ehh . . . you're too young yet to fully understand what I'm going to discuss with you. But whatever your feelings about what I am going to say, I want you to understand this; as your father, I want nothing more for you than a better and happy future; you and your sister.

APPEAH: Thank you, Father.

KUMI MENSAH: [*Confusedly*] A long time ago, . . . I was your age then . . . no much . . . younger . . . when my father . . . that is your grandfather . . . called me one dawn, as I have called you now . . . and . . . and . . . he told me a very delightful story. Would you like to hear the story?

APPEAH: Yes, I'll hear it.

KUMI MENSAH: Good. Once, there was a great competition between the lion and the ant . . . for a bag of gold and a slice of lime. Are you listening?

APPEAH: Yes . . .

KUMI MENSAH: Well . . . a lion, we all know, is a wily and strong animal. And so using the sheer virtue of his cunning and brutal strength, the lion was able to bully the ant and kept all the gold for himself. The ant reluctantly accepted the lime and went home. Now listen carefully to this part.

APPEAH: Yes . . .

KUMI MENSAH: When the ant got home, he found out that a great measles epidemic had broken out and his young one had contacted the measles. The lime was quickly applied and the ant was saved. But the lion . . ? We all know he is wily, wealthy and strong. But sometimes, too many good things can be bad! The lion found this out soon. When the lion got home, he found out that his young one had the measles too. All the lion needed was a tiny slice of lime . . . but where, I ask you could he find one? You see, that little lime, a worthless slice of lime, had become life itself; one can't cheat on or buy life. And so the lion and his young one both died, leaving all the gold, strength, and wiliness to the dust. That's how the world works. Sometimes our misfortunes are fortunes in themselves. I know you like going to school; I know you are doing well in school; I know all about your visions and future aspirations but . . . eh . . . I'm going to give you money to go and bring the rest of your things back home from school . . .

APPEAH: Why? Am I not going back to school again?

KUMI MENSAH: [Reaches for his pipe] I'm not stopping you from school. I only . . . [Lights pipe]

APPEAH: Why then? Father . . .

KUMI MENSAH: I wouldn't ask you to leave school if I didn't have to. You know yourself, these are very difficult times for all of us . . .

APPEAH: Father . . . I have only two more years to . . .

KUMI MENSAH: Difficult. Very difficult.

APPEAH: Only two years, Father . . .

KUMI MENSAH: In two years, if I'm cleared of this case, we shall consider your going back. At the moment, I can't afford to pay any more school fees. I must save money.

APPEAH: [With defiance] I can't leave school; never!

KUMI MENSAH: [Stands. In mild anger] I'm not asking you to consider leaving school; I'm ordering you to! I brought you into this world and you're going to do as I say! And that's final!

APPEAH: But Father, this is all my life. My future . . . it is my life . . .

KUMI MENSAH: I have nothing more to say about . . .

APPEAH: It is my future; my own future!

KUMI MENSAH: You don't want to understand my problems too! I'm locked up in a life-and-death fight for a precious property . . . LAND, A MONUMENT, LIFE itself! You're not asking me to throw away the life of the whole family to save you . . .

APPEAH: I heard your story, Father; but . . . I can't . . . I won't leave school.

KUMI MENSAH: The matter is closed. Tomorrow, you're going back to the school to bring the rest of your things home. [KUMI MENSAH *sees a shadow*] Who's there?

YAA ASI: It's me, Yaa Asi.

KUMI MENSAH: What are you doing there? How long have you been standing there?

YAA ASI: [*Entering*] I just entered, Father.

KUMI MENSAH: That's a lie! You're telling a lie! You've been eavesdropping!

YAA ASI: No, Father. I just came in . . .

KUMI MENSAH: What for? What do you want here?

YAA ASI: The . . . the broom . . .

KUMI MENSAH: There's no broom here!

YAA ASI: I . . . I . . .

KUMI MENSAH: Quick! Out! Out of here! [YAA ASI *exits through kitchen door*]

KUMI MENSAH: [*To* APPEAH] How long was that girl here?

APPEAH: [*Almost in tears*] I . . . I . . . don't . . .

KUMI MENSAH: I don't like the way that girl runs into every conversation in this house. She gossips too much. I'll warn her . . . [APPEAH *now weeping*] What's wrong with you there? Are you weeping?

APPEAH: [*Speaking through tears*] No . . . I . . . I . . .

KUMI MENSAH: Yes, you're weeping. What's the matter with you?

APPEAH: Nothing . . .

KUMI MENSAH: You're breaking a taboo! It's sacrilege for a son to weep on his father. Wipe those tears! [*Pause*] Wipe those tears, you hear me? [*Pause*] Appeah; you're going to slaughter a sheep! [APPEAH *wipes his tears*]

KUMI MENSAH: You wait until you take my place one day, then you'll understand my problems. Now, get ready! [*Picks the lamp and blows the light out*] It's daybreak. We must go to the farm. [*Exits*]

APPEAH *is alone, weeping.* YAA ASI *enters. Brother and sister look at each other, both weeping.*

YAA ASI: Appeah, stop weeping. Stop!

APPEAH: He's stopped me . . . he's . . . he's . . .

YAA ASI: He will change his mind.

APPEAH: It's that woman! She did . . . she . . . she . . .

YAA ASI: No use blaming it on anybody now . . . Listen; run to the headteacher and beg him to come and plead on your behalf . . .

APPEAH: He stopped me . . .

YAA ASI: You go to the headteacher . . .

APPEAH: Will that be of any help?

YAA ASI: Maybe. Father admires him; he could have some good influence.

APPEAH: I swear . . . I swear by my mother's coffin; if I'm stopped from school, I'll kill that woman . . . [*Crosses to the gate leading outside. Dog barking*]

VOICE: Hey . . . Somebody . . . hold that dog.

YAA ASI: Are you going to see the headteacher?

APPEAH: Yes. If Father asks about me, you haven't seen me!

YAA ASI: I'm praying for you, Appeah.

Exit APPEAH. *As he opens the gate, a man is entering. They crash into each other.* APPEAH *does not stop to look at him.*

Enter KWADWO OKOTO. *He is about thirty-five, excessively slim and fragile-looking. He undoubtedly is a heavy drinker. He is wearing an old and faded cloth and a pair of brown canvas shoes.*

KWADWO OKOTO: Oh I'm a dead man today . . .

YAA ASI: Get up!

KWADWO OKOTO: [*Getting up*] Head; my head . . . [*Pause*] And where is Appeah going in such a hurry?

YAA ASI: I don't know.

KWADWO OKOTO: Well. At least I'm here. [*Looks around*] Oh . . . I see Father has bought a new table. Must be a very expensive table.

YAA ASI: Did you come all the way here to see a table?

KWADWO OKOTO: No . . . no . . . no . . . [*Pause*] Well . . . ehh . . . Is my old man home? [*Grins*]

YAA ASI: Yes.

KWADWO OKOTO: Is he awake yet?

YAA ASI: You want to see him?

KWADWO OKOTO: Yes . . . But . . . but . . . don't call him yet. Just give me a chair. I'll sit and wait for him.

YAA ASI: You have a chair there. [*Pointing*]

KWADWO OKOTO: Where?

YAA ASI: There. Right there.

KWADWO OKOTO: No . . . not that one. That's for big men. I mean those men who made it in life. Give me something small . . . a kitchen stool will be fine.

YAA ASI: A chair is a chair. Sit on it.

KWADWO OKOTO: [*Nervously*] Well . . . if my old man's daughter says I must, I must. [*Sits*] Thanks. And how are you this morning?

YAA ASI: You selfish man! When you visit a house, you first express concern for your host before you ask for a chair for yourself.

KWADWO OKOTO: True. True. You're right. Quite right. [*Pause. Grins*]
Well . . . ehh . . . Where did you say Appeah was going?

YAA ASI: You ask too many questions. Why don't you . . .

KWADWO OKOTO: Please . . . please . . . I didn't mean to . . . I didn't
mean to . . . [*Pause. Beckons*] Yaa, come; come close. Here; I want to
ask you something.

YAA ASI: What is it?

KWADWO OKOTO: [*Spies around him before whispering into* YAA'S *ear*] Do you
know if your father has any cigarettes?

YAA ASI: I don't know.

KWADWO OKOTO: Go and find out. And if he has any, steal just two . . .
only two sticks for me. [*Enter* COMFORT. *In dog humility* KWADWO
OKOTO *covers up*] Good morning, Auntie.

COMFORT: Morning, Kwadwo. How are you?

KWADWO OKOTO: Just as usual, Auntie . . . the world won't stop lashing
hard at . . .

COMFORT: You don't have to stand up when you're talking to me . . . Sit
down.

KWADWO OKOTO: Well . . . eh . . . just to show respect to my father's
wife.

COMFORT: You are much older than I am, Kwadwo . . . [*To* YAA ASI]
Yaa Asi, get the bucket from the kitchen and fetch me some water for
my bath. I'm leaving for Accra this morning. [*Exit* COMFORT *into her
bedroom.* YAA ASI *makes for the kitchen door*]

KWADWO OKOTO: Yaa; hey Yaa! What about the cigarettes?

YAA ASI: Don't bother me! Don't you see Auntie . . .

KWADWO OKOTO: Ohh . . . please; please, don't shout! Don't shout! I'll
wait . . . I'm waiting . . . [KWADWO OKOTO *looks around him then
looks over himself. He spots a hole in the cloth he is wearing; puts his finger
through the hole and sighs*] Life oh life! What did man come to do
in this world at all, eh? [*He dips his hand into his pocket and produces a
crumpled stub of cigarette. Just as he puts the cigarette into his mouth,*
KUMI MENSAH *enters.* KWADWO OKOTO *jumps up from his chair; the stub
of cigarette falls on the floor. As he steps on the stub* . . .] Good morning,
Father . . .

KUMI MENSAH: Morning, Kwadwo. How are you today?

KWADWO OKOTO: [*Bows*] I'm fine, Father. I'm fine . . .

KUMI MENSAH: And your old woman; how is she?

KWADWO OKOTO: Awo is fine . . . very fine, Father.

KUMI MENSAH: Comfort told me you're here. Have you been waiting
long?

KWADWO OKOTO: Oh no, Father. I just came . . . . only a few seconds
ago . . .

KUMI MENSAH: I haven't seen you for months . . . Oh . . . sit down . . .
sit down.

KWADWO OKOTO: [*Sits*] Thank you, Father.

KUMI MENSAH: Have you come to see me about anything special?

KWADWO OKOTO: [*Stands*] Yes; Father . . . I came . . . [*Stops short*]

KUMI MENSAH: Sit down . . .

KWADWO OKOTO: Thank you, Father [*Sits*]

KUMI MENSAH: Well . . . [KWADWO OKOTO *attempts to stand up again*]
Sit; sit and speak. Well . . . I'm listening . . .

KWADWO OKOTO: I . . . came with a . . . a . . . [*Stops short*]

KUMI MENSAH: Go ahead; I'm listening to you. [*Pause*] Kwadwo, don't
waste my time this morning. I was going to the farm as you came in.

KWADWO OKOTO: [*Stands*] I'm . . .

KUMI MENSAH: Sit down! You are speaking to your own father. Besides,
you're not a small boy, you know.

KWADWO OKOTO: Well . . . eh . . . I came . . . I am involved in a little
trouble, Father.

Pause.

KUMI MENSAH: What little trouble?

KWADWO OKOTO: I have had a little case . . . some little trouble that
calls for Father's attention.

KUMI MENSAH: You still haven't said a thing. Why can't you be a man
and say what you want to say . . .

KWADWO OKOTO: It is about . . . Alice. I mean the daughter of the
kenkey seller living next to our house. I think you know the girl . . .

KUMI MENSAH: I know Alice. What about her?

KWADWO OKOTO: I was in my house yesterday evening when her mother
called on me. And she said . . . well . . . what I mean is . . . I have
been playing with the girl for sometime . . . and it seems . . . she's
changed colour a bit.

KUMI MENSAH: You mean she's pregnant?

KWADWO OKOTO: [*Scratching his hair*] It . . . it seems so . . .

KUMI MENSAH: What's the trouble in this? Get married. You're almost
thirty-five; you are too old to stay single, you know. Did you tell your
mother about it?

KWADWO OKOTO: Yes, Father.

KUMI MENSAH: What did she say?

KWADWO OKOTO: She . . . she asked me to come to you . . .

KUMI MENSAH: Why? Can't she handle this without me? This is no
problem case. Your mother can handle this.

KWADWO OKOTO: That's what I said too . . . but she . . . she said she's
only a woman; giving marriage is not part of her traditional
function.

KUMI MENSAH: Well, she's right. Well . . . Alice is in Form Four, am I
right?

KWADWO OKOTO: Yes, Father.

KUMI MENSAH: You know the consequences then?

KWADWO OKOTO: Yes . . .

KUMI MENSAH: Good. Did you bring any money?

KWADWO OKOTO: [*Jumps from chair and prostrates himself before* KUMI MENSAH] Father . . . have mercy on me.

KUMI MENSAH: Get up! Get up from the floor! Sit down and speak clearly; I want to hear you well. [*Pause*] [KWADWO OKOTO *speaking in an undertone*] Speak up! I don't hear a word of what you're muttering there! [*Pause*] You are at my what?

KWADWO OKOTO: I'm not working . . .

KUMI MENSAH: You are not working. Yes, I knew you were coming round to that. When I talk to you young men, I only talk to a piece of wood. I inherited your father, but how many times have I seen you in this house since your father died? Do you know my farm? For the past five years I have been going up and down on your own father's land case. You all know what I have been going through; and what I'm still going through. I need somebody around me sometimes; somebody I can share confidence and sometimes send to represent me when I am not well. It is my wife I have to send this morning. And you; all of you are around . . . you, and your brothers . . . Kofi Kwaateng, Asamoah Kwaku, Kwaku Takyi . . . four strong men; and you do nothing but sit in the streets, smoking and drinking and playing draughts and engaging yourselves in pointless arguments. Now that you have a pregnant girl on your hand, you suddenly remember that you have a father, and run here like a guinea fowl looking for shelter. Where do you expect me to go dig up that money to marry that girl for you? Do you think I bear money like a palm tree; or that I am a magician?

KWADWO OKOTO: [*Stands and bows*] I . . . don't mean to . . . offend you about this . . . it is not in a child's way to speak to his elders in proverbs . . . [*Kneels*] . . . but there is a popular saying: 'If you're made an elder, you're crowned with troubles.' I know I have wronged my father, but I am in trouble now. I beg my father to look at me as one of his strayed sons and come to my poor aid.

KUMI MENSAH: You young men of today think and take life too easy. Five hundred cedis headache; that's what you're asking me to bear for you. [*Calls*] Comfort! Comfort! What is that woman doing? [*Enter* COMFORT] Are you ready?

COMFORT: I'm not ready.

KUMI MENSAH: Hurry up then! I have to go to the farm!

COMFORT: Leave the money on the table!

KUMI MENSAH: I want to see you leave the house . . .

COMFORT: Okay, okay . . . I'll be ready soon.

[*Exit* CÓMFORT *into the bathroom*] [*Dog barking backstage*]

KUMI MENSAH: Appeah! Appeah!

KWADWO OKOTO: Appeah? He's not in the house.

KUMI MENSAH: Not in the house? Where is he?

KWADWO OKOTO: He's gone to the town.

KUMI MENSAH: To the town? What for?

KWADWO OKOTO: [*Bows*] I don't know, Father. I only crashed . . .

KUMI MENSAH: Yaa Asi! Yaa Asi! [*Enter* YAA ASI *from kitchen*] What's your brother going to do in town?

YAA ASI: I don't know, Father.

KUMI MENSAH: That boy! I asked him to get ready; we were going to the farm! What's he going to do in town! Alright go . . . go back to your work! [*Exit* YAA ASI]

KUMI MENSAH: Well . . . Kwadwo; what do you want me to do about this case? Eh . . . what do you want me to do? I don't have the money. You know I don't have any money.

KWADWO OKOTO: Father of fathers; saviour of saviours; a father I wipe my brow to; great Father on whom I lean for support, your son is caught up in a whirling storm. Kumi, the tall one; Kumi, the great one who saved 'Ofori' for 'Ofori' to save 'Sakyi', I am down on my knees to you. A man goes down on his knees only once in his life-time. I am on my knees before you today. Save me, kind Father, or your blood kin shall be made a slave.

KUMI MENSAH: This is how you young men go about inviting shame and disgrace on the whole family. What will other people say about us if . . . if the news got around that . . . you put that girl in a family way and . . . but . . . just . . . just dumped her off like . . . like . . . like some . . .

KWADWO OKOTO: I'm on my knees . . . In the name of the gods; the family and . . .

KUMI MENSAH: Up . . . get up! Sit down.

KWADWO OKOTO: Thank you, Father.

Pause.

KUMI MENSAH: Well . . . the damage is already done. The name and honour of the whole family is being questioned here. [*Pause*] Come with your mother tomorrow evening and we'll talk this matter over further. But you have to talk to your brothers. You must talk to them! If any of them come with any more such trouble, I won't stand for it, you hear? I won't stand for it!

KWADWO OKOTO: Yes, Father. I'll talk to them. Let me thank my father for . . .

KWADWO *stretches his hand ready to shake hands with* KUMI MENSAH. *The gate leading to town opens. Enter* KWAKU TWUM; *he is about* KWADWO OKOTO's *age. He is dressed up in a funeral cloth and chewing cola nut.*

KWADWO OKOTO: [*Leaving* KUMI MENSAH *in the cold*] Hey! Twum! What brings you here?

TWUM: I give you . . . good morning, Grandfather.

KUMI MENSAH: [*Shakes hands*] Thank you, Twum. [*Calls*] Yaa Asi; bring some drinking water . . .

TWUM: Thank you, Grandfather. But it's too cold a morning for water.

KUMI MENSAH: Kwadwo . . .

KWADWO OKOTO: Yes, Father . . .

KUMI MENSAH: Interpret! You'll tell our visitor we are all well and at peace here. It is he who has travelled.

KWADWO OKOTO: Ahh . . . Twum; that's what our 'chief' says; we are all well here and at peace. It is you who have come on a mission. If you are ready to speak, we're ready to hear you!

TWUM: Tell my grandfather I brought him a little sad news. Aberewatia, his sister and my grandmother, went to bed last night and slept deeply and in peace. In short, she's DEAD.

KWADWO OKOTO: How sad . . .

TWUM: The elders met and decided that this, my Grandfather, is your funeral. The whole family is gathered waiting for you to come over and bury your sister.

KUMI MENSAH: [*Highly agitated by the news*] Yaa Asi! Yaa Asi! [*Enter* YAA ASI] Get my black . . . polish my sandals; and get my new funeral cloth ready! Your mother died this morning; I'm leaving for the funeral.

KWADWO OKOTO: What did she die of? Has she not been well lately?

TWUM: She was not ill. We had all returned from the farm yesterday. There was nothing wrong with her; suddenly she started complaining about a little headache. That was all. We tried every herb we know of; we rubbed hot pepper into her eyes and put some into her nose; she didn't even blink or sneeze. So at dawn we sent for 'Okomfo' to help send her to her last peaceful sleep.

KWADWO OKOTO: My condolence . . . Twum . . .

KUMI MENSAH: [*Agitated*] Condolence? Condolence? Is that all you have to say? A very important member of the family is dead and all you do is sit there and express your feeling? Get ready for the funeral.

KWADWO OKOTO: [*Jumps up and prostrates himself before* KUMI MENSAH] Father; my thousand pardons! I . . . I . . . I . . . would do more than that if I could . . . but . . . my hands are tied . . . money . . . My father knows the poor man is despised even in precious clothes. My contribution at the funeral won't be as worthy as that of my father. Besides, [*Bows*] as the elders say, 'A father carries the burden of his children.' What you do at the funeral in your name, you do it for us, your children, as well. [*Enter* COMFORT *from the bathroom*]

KUMI MENSAH: [*Highly agitated*] Comfort . . . I have received sad news. My sister . . . my father's brother's daughter . . . died this morning. I must, for the funeral, immediately . . .

COMFORT: I knew it! I knew there was something foul in the air. I sneezed twice early in the morning. Now, I understand. [*Shakes hands with* TWUM] My condolence!

TWUM: Thank you, Auntie.

KUMI MENSAH: [*To* COMFORT] You . . . must come along with me. This is going to be a big funeral; a lot of very important people may attend . . . We have to provide well for our guests. You have to come along . . .

COMFORT: You want me to . . . ?

KUMI MENSAH: Not today. Go to my lawyer as planned. I'll give you more money to buy some of those expensive gins. This is a very big funeral. The eyes of the whole town will be on us. Everybody must go back home from the funeral with a good account of the family . . .

COMFORT: Yes . . . but who will take care of the house while we are away?

KUMI MENSAH: Appeah is home. He and his sister can take care of the house. And Kwadwo Okoto . . .

KWADWO OKOTO: [*Jumps up*] Yes, Father?

KUMI MENSAH: Kwadwo, you must stay and help keep an eye on things while I'm away.

KWADWO OKOTO: Everything is as good as taken care of.

KUMI MENSAH: What day is today?

KWADWO OKOTO: Wednesday.

KUMI MENSAH: And I have to travel for a funeral? Comfort, get me a bottle of schnapps. I must pour libation . . . [*Exit* COMFORT]

KUMI MENSAH: [*Highly excited*] Kwado Okoto . . . you must come and help watch the house while I'm away . . .

KWADWO OKOTO: [*Bows*] Your order is as good as done . . .

KWADWO OKOTO *winks at* TWUM, *mocking* KUMI MENSAH's *nervous excitement.* TWUM *is not amused. Enter* APPEAH *from the town.*

KUMI MENSAH: Where are you from Appeah?

APPEAH: [*Almost contrite*] Town.

KUMI MENSAH: What for? I told you we were going to the farm! What did you go to do in the town?

APPEAH: I . . .

KUMI MENSAH: Never mind. We have a funeral . . .

Enter MASTER ADOM.

KUMI MENSAH: Master! What a surprise visit! [MASTER ADOM *is one of the last of the missionary-looking Presbyterian village school headteachers. He is about fifty-five, a little bald and, in everything, a mark of simplicity*]

MR ADOM: Good morning, Mr Mensah.

KUMI MENSAH: You almost missed me. I'm just about ready to travel. One of my sisters died this dawn. It's a big funeral. Please sit down, Master. Kwadwo Okoto, give your chair to the master.

KWADWO OKOTO: Yes, Father. [*Gives chair to master*]

MR ADOM: Thank you. I don't really want to delay you that long. Appeah came to me this morning and . . . [*Sees* APPEAH *still hanging around*] Appeah, why don't you go and find something to do? I'll discuss this with your father, alone.

APPEAH: Yes, sir; Master.

MR ADOM: Well . . . eh . . . I was getting ready to have my bath . . . eh . . . to be precise . . . I was shaving, this morning, when Appeah was ushered in . . . It was such a big surprise to me because I didn't know Appeah was even home . . . [*Pause*]

KUMI MENSAH: Go on . . .

MR ADOM: I noticed he wasn't feeling too happy. Kind of near hysterics . . . and . . .

KUMI MENSAH: [*Trying to avoid what is afoot*] Master, I don't have much time today. I told you I am on my way to my sister's funeral. Why don't you come back some time . . .

MR ADOM: It won't take a minute . . . [*After a short pause*] Well . . . I was getting ready to go to Accra this morning, when Appeah came in weeping.

KUMI MENSAH: Weeping? Appeah weeping! [*Calls*] Yaa Asi! Yaa Asi!

MR ADOM: A moment . . . in a moment . . . [KUMI MENSAH *sits*] I'm not in any way trying to interfere in your family affairs . . .

KWADWO OKOTO: Master . . .

MR ADOM: Appeah came to tell me this morning that you stopped him from school . . .

KUMI MENSAH: [*In a fit of anger*] Did Appeah come to tell you that? Did he come to you with that?

MR ADOM: Mr Mensah . . .

KUMI MENSAH: Did Appeah come to you . . .?

MR ADOM: Don't be annoyed over this . . .

KUMI MENSAH: [*Suppressing his anger*] I'm not annoyed. No, I'm not! But I must tell you; that boy is . . . he is . . . [*Bursting out in anger*] Where is he! Where is that Appeah!

MR ADOM: Mr Mensah, I only . . .

KUMI MENSAH: [*Anger*] Where is that boy, Appeah! I want to see his face! Where is he? Let him come here and tell it to my face what he said I told him this morning! [*Calls*] Appeah! Appeah!

Enter COMFORT *with the schnapps.*

COMFORT: The schnapps . . .

KUMI MENSAH: [*Snatches the bottle from his wife and throws it away*] Where is that Appeah!

COMFORT: I'm not Appeah . . .

KUMI MENSAH: Where is he! Where is that hoodlum! That . . .

Enter APPEAH.

COMFORT: Here is your Appeah . . .

KUMI MENSAH: Appeah, what's that lie you've been spreading all over town about me?

MR ADOM: [*Helps* KUMI MENSAH *to chair*] Calm down, Mr Mensah . . .

KUMI MENSAH: [*Intoning*] That boy is a liar! A chronic liar! A . . . [*Pause*] [*Stands*] What did I tell you this morning? [*Pause*] I ask you! What did I tell you! Speak! Speak or I'll . . . [*Rushes to attack* APPEAH]

MR ADOM: Mr Mensah, you don't expect a child to speak up freely, after the way you have frightened him?

KUMI MENSAH: Frightened? He's not frightened yet! I'm settling this delinquency once and for all! Where's my cane? [*Picks cane from wall*] I'm not going to stomach any more of this nonsense from either you or your sister. Why do you children give me so much trouble like that? [*Wrestles with master as master snatches cane away from* KUMI MENSAH]

MR ADOM: Give me that cane. [*Throws cane away*]

KWADWO OKOTO: Appeah, tell your father what you have gone and said about him and everything . . .

KUMI MENSAH: If he doesn't speak, I'll slap his face right now! What did I tell you . . . [*Rushes on his son the second time.* KWADWO OKOTO, MASTER ADOM *and* TWUM *help restrain* KUMI MENSAH]

KWADWO OKOTO: Father . . . don't . . . it's enough . . .

MR ADOM: Please, Mr Mensah . . . don't!

TWUM: Grandfather . . . he begs . . .

KUMI MENSAH: He is a liar! I want him to understand that! He is a liar!

MR ADOM: If I may speak my mind freely, Mr Mensah, I don't see where Appeah lied in this case . . .

KUMI MENSAH: Are you implying that I am a liar?

MR ADOM: I'm not implying anything; I just don't see where Appeah could have lied in this matter. If you are actually stopping him from school . . .

KUMI MENSAH: Mr Adom, did you come here just to insult me?

MR ADOM: I just don't see the point about Appeah . . .

KUMI MENSAH: [*Inflamed*] Look here, Master, I wasn't born yesterday, understand? You don't have to press your left thumb to my nose and call me a fool before I know you are abusing me! You have been a good friend; I don't want to pick bones with you. Leave this house and that boy alone! This is my house and he is my son; I can do what I please with him . . .

MR ADOM: You are wrong, Mr Mensah. You think Appeah is your son so you can do what you please with him. But, you see, he is also a human being like you and me . . . and like everybody else has his own personal problems and ambitions. He is a member of a sprawling family alright but he is also himself and must be allowed to function as he is himself . . .

KWADWO OKOTO: [*Stands and bows*] I am not interrupting you, Master. But you know yourself, my old man is travelling. We must not waste too much of his time. In fact, I personally don't see what there is to talk about in this . . . Appeah, we all know, acted irrationally. He did what a child shouldn't have done. For a child to lie so blatantly about his own father is something one can't condone. Let's not argue about this any further. Let's rather help Appeah apologize and beg the old man . . .

MR ADOM: Beg him for telling the truth . . .

TWUM: [*Dogmatically*] Yes, Master . . . And I think you too must apologize to my grandfather. [*Stands and bows*] Excuse my saying this; I have no business speaking to my elders in proverbs, but permit this my discourtesy and crudeness. [*Bows*] There is a popular saying, 'If the elder lets out bad air in public, it is not for us, the children to laugh.' Whatever my grandfather discussed with Appeah shouldn't have gone out of this house. Let's help kill the whole case by begging my grandfather . . . And you, Master, have to apologize for . . .

MR ADOM: For what?

KUMI MENSAH: [*Stands*] Master, I think you've said all you want to say. Now, if you'll excuse me, I have a funeral . . .

MR ADOM: Is the dead now more important to you than the living?

KWADWO OKOTO: You don't bury your dead?

MR ADOM: Mr Mensah, please don't let this my little plea fall on deaf ears. Don't stop Appeah from school. I have known your son since he was a little child in my school. He is a brilliant boy with a bright future. Don't destroy this hope of the future of your own family. Cut off his education and you have cut off the future life of the family. One must have focus in what one sets out to do in life or . . . like a bat . . .

KUMI MENSAH: I must say, Master, I really resent the way you are trying to instruct me on how I must bring up my own children.

Enter COMFORT.

COMFORT: Yaa Asi has finished packing.

KUMI MENSAH: Give me five cedis. [COMFORT *gives him the money which he hands to* APPEAH] Here is money. Go and bring the rest of your things from the school . . . today! I said I was going to consider your going back to school after some time but after what you have done, it's all finished. You are not going to school any more! And that's final! You can complain to whoever you please! [*To the Headteacher*] Master, I think there is nothing more to discuss. I have to be on my way. [KUMI MENSAH *exits with* COMFORT. APPEAH *is left sobbing*]

KWADWO OKOTO: What is the matter with you, Appeah? Hey, what's wrong? Are you weeping? Excuse me, Master; do you have any cigarettes? [*Pause*] Master, any cig.?

MR ADOM: [*Hands over a packet*] Help yourself.

KWADWO OKOTO: [*Takes two sticks and pockets one*] Match? Any matches? [*Mimics the act of striking a match*]

MR ADOM: [*To* APPEAH] Don't give up home yet . . .

KWADO OKOTO: [*Makes a sign*] Master . . . any matches?

MR ADOM: [*To* APPEAH] Listen to me! Don't weep over this. It's still some weeks before your school opens. Something good might turn up . . . your father might change his mind.

Enter YAA ASI.

KWADWO OKOTO: Yaa Asi, get me a hot coal from the kitchen! [YAA ASI *ignores him*]

YAA ASI: [*To* APPEAH] Appeah . . . come in and . . .

KWADWO OKOTO: Yaa Asi, I asked you to get me a hot coal, didn't I?

APPEAH: [*In real anger; slaps* KWADWO OKOTO] Leave that girl alone! Yaa Asi! Yaa Asi! Yaa Asi! every day . . . every second of the day! Yaa Asi is not your slave!

KWADWO OKOTO: But . . . but . . . what did I say wrong?

Enter COMFORT.

APPEAH: [*Boiling with rage*] Yaa Asi is not a slave! And I'm not anybody's servant! You've all done your best to destroy us. Laugh! Laugh your head off! Laugh! Lazy people! Laugh at your lazy selves. Sit and laugh, lazy people! I'm not going to be your servant; and Yaa Asi is not going to be your slave. I'm not going to be anybody's slave! NEVER! [APPEAH *dashes out of the room. As he is about to exit he bumps into* AUNTIE COMFORT, COMFORT *is thrown off balance*]

COMFORT: [*Hurt*] What!

Blackout.

END OF ACT TWO

ACT THREE

Set: Same as in Act Two. Some months later. Early morning.
KWADWO OKOTO, *still in his old cloth, is sitting chain smoking.* YAA
ASI *is sweeping around the sitting room.*

KWADWO OKOTO: [*Commanding*] Here! This side! Sweep this side again.

YAA ASI: Get up! I have to sweep under the chair.

KWADWO OKOTO: [*Points*] This side first! Don't you see I'm relaxing?
   [*Puffs a thick cloud of smoke*]

YAA ASI: Get up or I'll hit you with the broom . . .

KWADWO OKOTO: Don't hit a man with a broom; it makes him impotent!

YAA ASI: Get up or I'll . . .

KWADWO OKOTO: [*Snatches the brown and throws it away*] Give me that! I
   have only one child. And mind how you speak to me these days. I am
   a father now, you know. [*Dog barking*]

YAA ASI: [*Picks up broom*] Some father.

KWADWO OKOTO: [*Sits*] I am a father alright. I can command children
   now. Hurry! Sweep here again! And all over the compound.

Gate opens. Enter a strange woman. She is about KWADWO OKOTO'S *age. She is
dressed from head to toe in red with deep red lipstick. She is fat with jet black
smooth skin but with bleached brown face. She is smoking an almost finished cigarette.*

KWADWO OKOTO: Hey Yaa . . . hold the dog!

YAA ASI: [*Crosses and shuts the gate on the dog*] Please, come in! It won't hurt
   you.

AUNTIE AYELE: Thank you . . . [*Throws cigarette away*]

KWADWO OKOTO: Hey Yaa. Bring a chair. Hurry!

AUNTIE AYELE: Thank you. May I have a drink of water?

KWADWO OKOTO: Quick, Yaa; some water!

AUNTIE AYELE: I don't like dogs. They make me nervous. May I?
   [*Accepts cigarette from* KWADWO OKOTO]

KWADWO OKOTO: Only one left but . . . help yourself.

AUNTIE AYELE: [*Lights up the cigarette and puffs away*] That's good! Maybe
   you can help me. I am looking for the house of Mr Mensah . . .
   Kumi Mensah.

KWADWO OKOTO: You are right in his house.

AUNTIE AYELE: Are you Mr Mensah?

KWADWO OKOTO: [*Pompously*] Kwadwo Okoto. Mr Kwadwo Okoto.

Enter YAA ASI *with the water.*

YAA ASI: Here is the water.

AUNTIE AYELE: [*Gives cigarette to* KWADWO OKOTO] Thank you.
[*Drinks and gives cup back to* YAA ASI] [*Exit* YAA ASI]

AUNTIE AYELE: That's Appeah's sister, right?

KWADWO OKOTO: You know Appeah?

AUNTIE AYELE: Very well. But it is his father I want to see. Where is he?

KWADWO OKOTO: He has gone to Accra.

AUNTIE AYELE: And Appeah?

KWADWO OKOTO: Appeah?

AUNTIE AYELE: Yes, Appeah. Where is he?

KWADWO OKOTO: He disappeared from this house, months ago.

AUNTIE AYELE: Sc that is what it is all about. Thank you for the
cigarette . . . [*Gets up*]

KWADWO OKOTO: Wait!

AUNTIE AYELE: Never mind. Thank you for the water . . . [*Exits*]

YAA ASI: Kwadwo . . .

Re-enter AUNTIE AYELE.

AUNTIE AYELE: When is Mr Mensah coming back home?

KWADWO OKOTO: About ten. Why?

AUNTIE AYELE: I'll be back . . .

KWADWO OKOTO: Wait a minute! I don't even know your name.

AUNTIE AYELE: Auntie Ayele. An old friend . . .

KWADWO OKOTO: An old friend of Appeah.

AUNTIE AYELE: Yes . . . Appeah; and I am coming back. [*Exits*]

KWADWO OKOTO: [*Exclaiming*] Huem! That's a real horse-power. My
brother is really tough . . .

YAA ASI: Kwadwo . . .

KWADWO OKOTO: Yes . . .

YAA ASI: Don't you see?

KWADWO OKOTO: See what?

YAA ASI: That's a policewoman.

KWADWO OKOTO: She is a red-light woman.

YAA ASI: She is a policewoman.

KWADWO OKOTO: A loose woman!

YAA ASI: A policewoman.

KWADWO OKOTO: I don't have to argue with you. Go! Go finish your
work!

Enter COMFORT *from bedroom.*

COMFORT: Yaa Asi, don't forget to sweep the compound today. Your
father is coming back this afternoon.

Exit YAA ASI *into her bedroom.*

KWADWO OKOTO: This morning.

COMFORT: It's you Kwadwo! You're here early today. Any special news?

KWADWO OKOTO: I came to help welcome my old man.

COMFORT: At last! I've prayed all night for three days. The gods be with us.

KWADWO OKOTO: The gods are always with those who know how to fight for what is their own. I have seen nothing but good luck signs this morning.

COMFORT: By the way, how is your wife this morning?

KWADWO OKOTO: God! I wish you hadn't mentioned her!

COMFORT: Still fighting each other as usual?

KWADWO OKOTO: Nooooo . . . Auntie!

COMFORT: I sensed something.

KWADWO OKOTO: Ohh . . . Noooo . . .

COMFORT: I told you . . . I told . . . I'm more than a witch. You can't hide a secret from me. I can smell out deep secrets like the red ant. Your wife's had a baby. And I am even going to make a guess: [*Pause*] It's a girl!

KWADWO OKOTO: A boy! At first cockcrow today that poor girl finally unloaded her burden on me!

COMFORT: [*Embracing* KWADWO OKOTO] Congratulations! Oh, I'm so happy for you.

KWADWO OKOTO: Happy? Happy? For the woman . . . I have to bear all the headache from now. This is the time when the real man dips his hand in his pocket and pulls out 'the cash'. But where does one find money to play a good father, these days?

COMFORT: The gods will provide. [*Crosses to bedroom door*] Tell your wife, I'll come down and see her as soon as things are settled in the house. Today is . . . [*Re-enter* YAA ASI *from bedroom*] Yaa Asi; have you finished with your work? [*Exit* YAA ASI *through gate leading outside into town*] Hey . . . where are you going? [YAA ASI *does not answer*] [*To* KWADWO OKOTO] You see that? You see? When that girl's father is not in the house, she crowns herself the reigning queen. Look how everything is junked up here and she's going, where, nobody knows . . . I wouldn't be surprised if she, one of these days, became like her brother . . .

KWADWO OKOTO: You remind me! A girl friend of Appeah was here looking for him.

COMFORT: A girl friend? Here? In this house?

KWADWO OKOTO: Right here!

COMFORT: Was she alright?

KWADWO OKOTO: She was a bit drunk.

COMFORT: [*Crosses to* KWADWO OKOTO] [*Gossiping*] One of the city 'gangsters' alright. You heard about that gang called 'The Canoe Boys'? Appeah is said to be an active member of that gang. Shocking.

KWADWO OKOTO: Appeah could have found himself a decent job at least. With all the schools he attended, he should easily find a respectable job in the city.

COMFORT: Ha! Appeah up to some good? You've never met a more lazy and evil-minded hypocrite . . .

KWADWO OKOTO: I always thought him shy and hard-working and . . .

COMFORT: Ṣly and a hypocrite; that's the word. Such boys never end up any better in life . . .

KWADWO OKOTO: [Shocked] Auntie! Don't curse a child on Wednesday morning. Any curse from a human mouth that's bitten pepper and salt can come true. Let's not say such a thing; especially on Wednesday morning. After all he is your husband's son; if he falls into disgrace, it will touch you too . . . in fact all of us.

COMFORT: If that is his aim . . . to put the whole family to shame, then he's got to think again. Because, you see, the family can disown him; can disinherit him. And why not? What use has anybody for a boy who can run away from his own father for no reason at all?

KWADWO OKOTO: Well, you're right. I was bypassed for my own father's inheritance . . .

COMFORT: Quiet! I think I hear somebody coming this way . . .

KWADWO OKOTO: I don't hear anything . . . oh, yes, you're right! Yes . . . here . . . [Disappointed] . . . It's the master!

COMFORT: What does he want?

KWADWO OKOTO: Who knows? [Sits]

Silence, as the two look at each other. A moment later, MR ADOM enters. He is carrying a copy of the day's newspaper.

MR ADOM: Morning, Comfort.

COMFORT: Morning.

MR ADOM: Is your husband home?

KWADWO OKOTO: Hey, Master, you didn't greet . . .

MR ADOM: I'm sorry . . . Morning, Kwadwo . . .

KWADWO OKOTO: Mr Kwadwo . . . Mr Kwadwo Okoto!

COMFORT: Sit down, Master.

MR ADOM: Thank you. Is your husband . . .?

COMFORT: [Cuts the master off short] He left for Accra. How are your wife and the children?

MR ADOM: They are all well. My wife sends her greetings.

KWADWO OKOTO: [Gets up] Auntie, maybe you and the master want to discuss about something private. I'll wait in the kitchen.

COMFORT: Sit down. You are a father now, you know.

MR ADOM: Has your wife delivered, Kwadwo?

KWADWO OKOTO: [Sits] Yes, Master . . . early today; at dawn. She unloaded her whole burden on me alright.

MR ADOM: A burden eh? A real burden that you and I were born to bear.

KWADWO OKOTO: You and I?

MR ADOM: Well . . . don't ask me to call you Mister Kwadwo Okoto. Not yet. Because these days the man who brings forth a child does not automatically become the father of the child unless he does his duty by maintaining the child also. So don't call yourself a father yet . . . and you are not a mister until . . .

COMFORT: I thought you came to see us?

MR ADOM: I came to see your husband. I'll come back . . . maybe. Or better still, give him this newspaper . . .

COMFORT: Anything special in the paper?

MR ADOM: Just give him that! [*Exits*]

KWADWO OKOTO: This master and his stingy, selfish self! Always advising . . . and half the time I don't even understand what he talks about . . .

COMFORT: Can you read a newspaper, Kwadwo?

KWADWO OKOTO: I believe I can spell a few words, alright.

COMFORT: [*Gives him the newspaper*] Here. Try and see if you can read it. The master wanted to tell us something but . . . I think I know what! Kwadwo, we have won the court case!

KWADWO OKOTO: Won it?

COMFORT: Yes. The master read about it in the newspaper. That's why he wouldn't say anything. He's always been wishing that we lose this case. Because, he thinks we stopped Appeah from school because of this land case . . .

KWADWO OKOTO: You are right! [*Trying to read*] Let me see. It's been more than ten years since I read anything. (Spelling) A – C – C – R – A; Accra.

COMFORT: Kwado . . . Look!

KWADWO OKOTO: What?

COMFORT: The back of the newspaper. It's Appeah!

KWADWO OKOTO: It's the picture of Appeah alright! Well, my brother in the papers. And he's smiling too; he must have fallen into some big fortune.

COMFORT: Where is Yaa Asi? She must read it for us.

KWADWO OKOTO: [*Fumbling with the paper*] Let me try, again. I'll read it this time. I'll read it . . . [*Spelling*] A; B – O – Y, Boy . . . ; C – O – N . . . this is what I call 'university words' . . . C – O – N . . .

YAA ASI *enters from the town. She is carrying* KUMI MENSAH'S *travelling bag.*

COMFORT: [*Harshly*] Where are you coming from?

YAA ASI: [*Almost contrite*] Town.

COMFORT: [*Sees the bag*] Is that your father's bag?

YAA ASI: Yes.

COMFORT: Where is he himself?

YAA ASI: On the cross-road. He's talking with the master . . .

COMFORT: Okay. Let me have the bag. And go and prepare some food. Your father must be hungry. [*Exits with the bag into bedroom*]

KWADWO OKOTO: [*Beckons* YAA ASI] Yaa, come here.

YAA ASI: What do you want?

KWADWO OKOTO: Over here. I want to ask you something.

YAA ASI: Okay. What is it?

KWADWO OKOTO: Did your father say anything about the land case? I mean . . . has he won it? The case . . . you know what I mean . . .

YAA ASI: I don't know, Kwadwo . . .

KWADWO OKOTO: No sign of anything? Is he wearing anything . . . anything white?

YAA ASI: A white handkerchief on his left wrist. Yes.

KWADWO OKOTO: [*Jumps from chair*] Thank you . . . thank you . . . thank you very much. [*Exclaims*] WON! VICTORY! VICTORY!

Enter COMFORT.

COMFORT: What's wrong here?

KWADWO OKOTO: [*Jumps*] VICTORY!

COMFORT: What's the matter, Kwadwo?

KWADWO OKOTO: [*Embraces* COMFORT] I have won! Won! Won! [*Runs out*] Victory! Victory!

COMFORT: What's the matter with him?

YAA ASI: Don't know.

COMFORT: [*Looks around*] Wait! Where did I leave that newspaper?

YAA ASI: Kwadwo has . . .

COMFORT: No! He shouldn't have taken that paper away! He will spread the news all over the town. A pack of envious degenerates! He and his brothers won't look for any decent work! Sitting around all day watching and expecting heaven to send down salt and honey! Lazy men! And they have the nerve to think they deserve a share of every penny one makes in this house! [*Sees* YAA ASI *looking at her in cold mockery*] What are you standing there waiting for?

YAA ASI: [*In mild anger*] You asked me to wait!

COMFORT: Go! Go to your work! I only wanted you to read something in the newspaper but . . .

YAA ASI: Father is here . . .

COMFORT: Are you still in this room? Or do you want me to shout my lungs off before you hear me?

YAA ASI: [*Rebels*] I'm going! Why do you want to shout at every . . . [YAA ASI *takes sharp turn*] [*Exits*]

A moment later KUMI MENSAH *enters. He has a white handkerchief around his left wrist. His face is very pale and wears something between a worried and solemn look.*

COMFORT: Oh, at last! Here . . . here; you look tired.

KUMI MENSAH: Was it Yaa Asi I heard shouting?

COMFORT: Sit here. You're tired . . . [*Calls*] Yaa Asi, bring your father some good drinking water.

KUMI MENSAH: Is she alright?

COMFORT: Who?

KUMI MENSAH: Yaa Asi.

COMFORT: You look tired, K . . .

KUMI MENSAH: [*Shouting*] I'm not tired!

COMFORT: But . . . but . . . what did I say wrong?

Silence.

KUMI MENSAH: Where is the newspaper?

COMFORT: [*Gets up and rushes to kitchen door*] Yaa Asi, will you please hurry up with the water!

KUMI MENSAH: Where is that newspaper?

COMFORT: But why? Why the shouting!

KUMI MENSAH: Where is the paper?

COMFORT: Kumi! What is wrong? What is it?

KUMI MENSAH: [*Stressing every word*] Where is the newspaper?

COMFORT: Kwadwo Okoto was trying to read it a moment ago. He must still have it. Oh, before I forget, Kwadwo's wife had a baby boy early this dawn.

Enter YAA ASI *with the water.*

KUMI MENSAH: [*Trying not to look at* YAA ASI] I don't need any water, Yaa.

COMFORT: You must pour libation . . .

KUMI MENSAH: [*Shouting*] Take the water away!

COMFORT: Okay, take it away. If he wants to break a sacred taboo . . .

KUMI MENSAH: [*To* YAA ASI] I wasn't shouting at you, Yaa . . .

YAA ASI: Yes . . . Father . . .

Pause.

KUMI MENSAH: Have you received any bad news from the family at home?

YAA ASI: All is . . .

COMFORT: The sheep was brought down yesterday morning.

KUMI MENSAH: Yaa Asi . . . sit down. [*Pause*] Sit down; please . . . Have you heard the news about your brother?

YAA ASI: No, Father.

KUMI MENSAH: A big disgrace. A big blot on the whole family . . . MY NAME!

COMFORT: Anything wrong?

KUMI MENSAH: Everything is wrong! Everything the good name of the family stood for . . .

COMFORT: What . . . what is it? What happened?

KUMI MENSAH: Appeah was sent to prison . . .

COMFORT: Prison?

KUMI MENSAH: Worse!

COMFORT: What is it, Kumi? Is he dead . . .?

KUMI: Yaa.

YAA ASI: Yes, Father . . .

KUMI MENSAH: I have good lawyers. I FOUGHT BEFORE AND I CAN FIGHT AGAIN! I will get Appeah out of prison! I AM STILL THE HEAD OF THE FAMILY: I WON'T LET ANYBODY DOWN . . .

YAA ASI: Father, Auntie wants me to prepare some porridge . . . Can I go now . . . ?

KUMI MENSAH: I'm talking to you. Or . . . aren't you interested in what I'm saying?

COMFORT: That's very rude of you, Yaa.

KUMI MENSAH: Leave that girl alone! I don't want you interfering in anything between me and my children again . . .

COMFORT: Are you talking to me?

KUMI MENSAH: Yaa Asi . . .

YAA ASI: [Speaking through tears] Yes . . . Father . . .

COMFORT: Kumi, were you talking to me!

KUMI MENSAH: Stop that, Yaa! Have confidence in me. Tomorrow, early tomorrow, you and I will go to Accra to see my lawyer.

YAA ASI: Thank you, father.

KUMI MENSAH: You have some complaints you want to . . .?

YAA ASI: No . . .

KUMI MENSAH: You have anything else you want to talk to me about?

YAA ASI: No.

KUMI MENSAH: Nothing at all?

YAA ASI: No.

KUMI MENSAH: You'd like to see Accra? You have never seen the sea before, have you?

YAA ASI: No.

KUMI MENSAH: We will go to the lawyer. Later, I can take you to see the sea. You would like to see the sea, wouldn't you?

YAA ASI: Well . . .

KUMI MENSAH: Good! Then let's have a little smile in your face. Smile. Smile a little. And have confidence in me. You still have a father . . .

YAA ASI: [Weeping] I must go . . . [Rushes out]

KUMI MENSAH: Alright! Alright . . . you may go . . . I'll call you again . . . soon . . .

Silence.

COMFORT: [Sternly] What ever is the matter with you? You want to humiliate me before that girl?

KUMI MENSAH: [To himself] God! Just when I thought it was all over . . . suddenly a man has to start fighting all over again . . .

COMFORT: It's about time you stood up and started behaving like a real man! What's all this impotence again? Because one boy of a whole large family is sent to prison? Did you send anybody to steal anything?

KUMI MENSAH: I pushed Appeah to that . . . pushed the child too far.

COMFORT: The master must have been pushing things in you. Look, Kumi, you are a man, a real man. Be strong; stand on your own two feet. Don't allow people to push ideas into you. You must know what is good for you and what the family's priority is. One boy is gone to prison but the whole family life must go on.

KUMI MENSAH: Comfort, do you know what a good name means to us?

COMFORT: The name of the family has suffered nothing . . . Simply act wisely! DISINHERIT HIM! Disown him! Prohibit Appeah the use of the family name and you're cleared of all embarrassments.

KUMI MENSAH: It's not that simple. Appeah is still my own son. He is attached to me through the SPIRIT that links a father to his son. That is the essence of family relations. Name is just a label . . . an identity. I can change a name but I can't alter the truth of the BLOOD THAT LINKS APPEAH TO HIS MOTHER AND THE SPIRIT THAT LINKS ME TO MY SON.

COMFORT: [Crosses almost into bedroom] Excuses! Excuses! Flimsy excuses!

KUMI MENSAH: [Calls] Yaa . . .

COMFORT: She is cooking breakfast.

KUMI MENSAH: You should be doing the cooking. Why must that girl be made to do everything in this house? What did I marry you for? [Calls] Yaa Asi . . .

COMFORT: [Crosses to KUMI MENSAH] Look, Kumi, I shall not be blamed for all the misfortunes in your children's life. Did I send Appeah to steal anything?

KUMI MENSAH: [Calls] Yaa Asi . . .

YAA ASI: [Off] I'm coming . . . Father . . .

COMFORT: Look here, Kumi, I'm your wife. If you . . .

YAA ASI comes rushing into room holding her travelling bag. Tries to hide the bag.

KUMI MENSAH: What are you hiding there behind you?

YAA ASI: [Drying her tears] My bag.

KUMI MENSAH: Why? Are you travelling?

YAA ASI: I want to go to my uncle for . . .

KUMI MENSAH: [Paternalistic] No! You are not going anywhere! Nowhere! Not while I'm still in this house!

YAA ASI: I want to go to my uncle . . .

KUMI MENSAH: Go, put away the bag. We shall talk later . . .

YAA ASI: I am going to my uncle . . . today.

KUMI MENSAH: [Shouting] You are not going ANYWHERE! [Pause] I wasn't shouting at you. [Pause] Put your things away and wait till tomorrow finds us. If you still wish to go, I myself, I'll take you to your uncle.

YAA ASI: I'm going to my uncle.

KUMI MENSAH: You can't travel today. It's Wednesday. Wednesdays are not propitious days for travellers.

YAA ASI: I'll travel.

KUMI MENSAH: Sit down. Sit down for a minute . . .

YAA ASI: I want to go to my uncle.

KUMI MENSAH: Alright. You'll go to your uncle . . . tomorrow. Stay with me just for tonight. I'll send you to your uncle tomorrow. You can stay with him for some time. Even if you want to continue with your schooling, I can arrange for that. Have confidence in your father.

YAA ASI: [*Weeping*] Yes . . .

KUMI MENSAH: You are weeping. Why . . . Yaa. Why?

YAA ASI: I want to go to my uncle . . .

KUMI MENSAH: [*Gives her the white handkerchief*] Here . . . use this. And, please, don't weep on your father. You are not an orphan.

YAA ASI *weeps freely.*

COMFORT: I hear voices. Yaa, stop weeping! We have visitors.

KUMI MENSAH: Visitors? [*Desperate*] Will you stop weeping! And remove your hands from the back of your head; it attracts trouble!

Gate opens. Enter KWADWO OKOTO *and his mother* AWO *from town.*

KUMI MENSAH: Go into your room! Quick! Into your room! And your bag with you! And hurry! Hurry!

Exit YAA ASI. AWO *is fully in view. She is already mumbling something to herself.* AWO *is about seventy-five. She is smoking from a clay pipe.*

KUMI MENSAH: [*Trying to compose himself*] Awo, I wasn't expecting you here.

AWO: [*To* KWADWO OKOTO] Eh? What did he say?

KWADWO OKOTO: [*Loudly*] He said he wasn't expecting you here!

AWO: I don't care if he wasn't expecting me. I'm here. Give me a chair . . . [*To* KWADWO OKOTO] . . . Get me a chair, goat! [COMFORT *quickly provides a chair*]

COMFORT: Sit down, Grandmother.

AWO: [*Sitting*] Ohhh . . . my waist! [*Shouting at* KWADWO OKOTO] Don't stand there looking like a goat! Sit down! It's all because of you I had to walk all this distance. Hey Kumi, is that the family stool you're sitting on?

KWADWO OKOTO: Mother, we have not greeted my father . . .

AWO: What? Speak up!

KWADWO OKOTO: We have not greeted father!

AWO: I know! You think I've forgotten myself?

KWADWO OKOTO: Nobody said you've forgotten yourself . . .

AWO: I wasn't born yesterday, Kwadwo . . .

KWADWO OKOTO: [*In anger*] You and your . . .

KUMI MENSAH: Don't argue with your mother, Kwadwo!

KWADWO OKOTO: [*Stands up and bows*] I heard you, Father.

AWO: And what is he saying there? What is he mumbling about? Speak out! Speak out if you think yourself a man!

COMFORT: It's alright, Awo.

AWO: Ho! But what is all this? If youthful pride were wealth, then everyone has had it in his lifetime.

KUMI MENSAH: Awo, don't . . . any more.

AWO: All right! All right! I'll shut my big mouth. [*To* KWADWO OKOTO] Get up! We have to greet your father.

KWADWO OKOTO: [*Shakes hands*] Morning and welcome, Father.

KUMI MENSAH: Thank you.

AWO: [*Struggling to stand up*] This chair is too low.

KUMI MENSAH: Don't worry getting up . . .

AWO: I must! [COMFORT *helps her to* KUMI MENSAH] I want to feel the steel palm of the man who has just thrown his enemy right off his feet! [*She shakes hands with* KUMI MENSAH *with incantations of ancestral blessings* (*The choice and length of the incantation is the director's choice.*) *She is helped back to her chair*] [*Sitting down*] Ahhhhh . . . this waist.

KUMI MENSAH: Comfort get us some good drinking water. [*Exit* COMFORT] This is a surprise visit. My old woman has not been to this house for nearly two years.

AWO: Eh! What did you say?

KWADWO OKOTO: He said he's not seen you in this house for more than two years.

AWO: I know! Ahh . . . I think I'm growing old. When I was a young girl, [*Shows her legs*] you see, I had such strong and beautiful legs. I was then coming here twice every day.

KUMI MENSAH: You could have sent Kwadwo to call me, Awo.

AWO: It is the bird that is hungry that travels. But where is my grandchild, Yaa Asi?

KUMI MENSAH: She is in her room.

AWO: Why? Is she not feeling well?

KUMI MENSAH: A little headache, that's all.

AWO: [*Grins*] Headache? [*Laughs*] No . . . no; you don't fool me. At Yaa Asi's age, every girl complains freely of headache. But the truth of it is, it is not the head at all. It is always in the stomach. That girl, I tell you, is of age! I met her at the market last week. I looked at her . . . and looked at her again. Then I asked myself: am I growing too old or am I seeing a stranger? That little crying baby I knew only yesterday has shot up as sweet and fresh as a young plantain stalk. Hmmm . . . the way girls grow up these days. [*Pause*] Kumi, what are you waiting for? You must find a husband for the girl. Don't wait too

long. The young men, these days; they are too wild! Well . . . don't
say I didn't warn you.

KWADWO OKOTO: Mother, Father is ready to welcome us . . .

AWO: What? Speak up; speak up like a man!

KWADWO OKOTO: Father is ready to welcome us here!

AWO: Let him. Do I have his hand? Or have I tied his hands behind him!

KUMI MENSAH: [*Shakes hands with* AWO] Welcome to my humble home,
Awo.

AWO: Thank you.

KUMI MENSAH: I hope you are all well at home.

AWO: Let him. Do I have his hand? Or have I tied his hands behind him?
me right up to my neck. And that same Kwadwo Okoto too! He won't
stop adding to my problems. I tell you, Kumi, these four foolish boys
of mine, they're simply walking on the back of my very neck!
[KUMI MENSAH *cuts in*]

KUMI MENSAH: Ah, Kwadwo, tell your mother, we are all well here. I've
just arrived from Accra . . . you see. I haven't even changed yet. As
we all know, the case was to be decided yesterday but it wasn't until
this morning that the law officers were ready to come to a decision.
And by the help of the gods, the Court found we are in the right. So I
hurried back here to report to the family . . . It was in the town that
I heard your wife has had a child.

AWO: [*Smoking*] Uuuuuuuuuuuuhhhhhmmmmmmm . . . At dawn, this
dawn!

KUMI MENSAH: . . . I was going to find something to eat and come down
and see you. Matter of fact, I wasn't expecting you here . . .

KWADWO OKOTO: . . . Mother, that's what . . .

AWO: I heard what he said! You've never learned to be a good
interpreter anyway. Help me up! Help me up! GOAT! Kumi,
you've lived up to the true name of the family. You have certainly
proved yourself like our predecessors. I know our ancestral spirit is
always guiding you. And your father; Oh, he was such a man! But
death, death loves to take only the best among men. He was cut off,
just in his prime. You were too young then to see how his ghost
haunted his killers. A powerful god had to be invited to drive his
spirit away from this house. But I know he is still with us . . . he has
always been. Any time we pour libation he hears us and comes to us.
[*Incanting*] Well done, Kumi. Well done; the son of a man! You have
proved yourself your father's son. May many . . . many more years
come and find you.

KUMI MENSAH: Thank you.

AWO: To the gods. To the gods only. Our thanks to the gods. They can
give, and they can take away. We live to do their wish.

KUMI MENSAH: I am a little tired. You came to see me about something?

AWO: What did you say? You must speak out loud sometimes you know.

I'm not exactly deaf but sometimes, when the wind blows into my left ear, I don't think I hear very well.

KWADWO OKOTO: He said, 'Did you come to see him about something?'

AWO: Of course, I came to see him about something! You know that, don't you?

KWADWO OKOTO: I was only telling you what he said . . .

AWO: But you know we came to see him about something . . .

KUMI MENSAH: Now, if I may know what it is all about . . . I am a little tired . . .

AWO: It's all about this same Kwadwo Okoto! Kumi, this boy here; he's my only headache left in this world!

KUMI MENSAH: What is it about this time, Kwadwo?

Enter COMFORT.

AWO: Oh, Fonkorrttee! I didn't see you when I came in.

COMFORT: I helped you into your chair.

AWO: You did? Ahhh . . . I must be getting old alright.

COMFORT: [*Humouring*] You're not old, Grandmother.

AWO: I know.

KUMI MENSAH: Oh, I'm so tired . . . Comfort; I was discussing something with Awo . . .

COMFORT: I'm leaving . . .

KUMI MENSAH: You don't have to.

COMFORT: I am. [*Exits*]

AWO: Is your wife annoyed?

KUMI MENSAH: She has a bad temper sometimes.

AWO: But you shouldn't allow that! You're the man! You should never allow a woman to show her temper in front of you. Ahhh, that's what I'm saying. The world is coming to an end! How can a wife dare spite a husband? Who's ever heard of such a thing? In my days, she would be made to slaughter a sheep, a whole sheep, right this minute.

KWADWO OKOTO: Mama, my old man is waiting to listen to our mission.

AWO: What did you say?

KWADWO OKOTO: 'Akora' is listening to us!

AWO: I know! And don't you tell me what I should do! You yourself . . . you should have made bold and told your father all yourself! It concerns you . . . and you alone!

KWADWO OKOTO: [*Rebelling*] I won't be picked on and tossed about anymore! It was your idea in the first place! I am . . .

KUMI MENSAH: Kwadwo Okoto, don't speak pointing your left finger at your mother!

KWADWO OKOTO: [*Bows*] With all respect for you, Father. But my mother is squeezing the very life out of me! Whatever she wants of me I don't know . . . she just keeps hounding me . . . everybody . . . day and night . . .

AWO: And I am a witch. A big red witch. Add that too! I am the old witch who's been responsible for all the misfortunes in your life . . .

KUMI MENSAH: Did you say that to your mother . . .

KWADWO OKOTO: [*In anger*] I'm leaving!

KUMI MENSAH: Sit down! Sit down there!

KWADWO OKOTO: Yes, Father . . .

KUMI MENSAH: If it is true you've been accusing your mother of witchcraft, then you have a very serious case to answer to the elders. As long as I am still the head of the family, such blatant disrespect for the old will not be condoned! Speak now, Awo. I shall hear your complaints.

AWO: Complaints? What complaints? I didn't come here to complain!

KUMI MENSAH: I shall hear whatever you came down with. It's about time I put a little squeeze on these children to remind them that they are not free to make a mess of their life and expect me always standing ready . . . waiting and ever ready to bail them out! I shall hear you, Awo.

AWO: Ah, well . . . Kumi, it's about nothing that is difficult. You know Kwadwo Okoto . . . that blockhead; he too is a father now and he will need some property to hold on to. You know too that all the lands around this area are barren, so barren even a goat won't eat the grass on them. We consulted some elders about this and they share the view that since it was Kwadwo's father who cleared the land and planted the cocoa on the farm that was in dispute, Kwadwo Okoto, as my eldest son and the rightful successor to his father, has a share in the cocoa farm. We therefore came here to ask you that since the dispute is over and the farm is now in the hands of the family, it should be handed over to Kwadwo and my children . . . the rightful owners of the farm.

KUMI MENSAH: What is it you're telling me, Awo? You mean you came down . . .

AWO: Speak up!

KUMI MENSAH: You mean, you came down to tell me you're here to claim the farm I have been fighting for all these years. And on the very day that I won . . .

AWO: We are not claiming anything. We are asking . . . MERELY asking that the farm be given to the rightful owners. Or is that a sin?

KUMI MENSAH: And who are the rightful owners?

AWO: My children. It was their father's property, wasn't it?

KUMI MENSAH: It was my brother's farm too . . .

AWO: A father's property passes on to his children. My children can't claim your property from Appeah, can they?

KUMI MENSAH: But . . . but . . . No! I'm not . . . [*Sudden anger*] How dare anybody . . . how dare any of you even think of a such a thing! You

. . . Kwadwo, how dare . . . you dare come to my face to . . . to . . . Stand up! Stand! On your two feet! I want to hear you say that again!

AWO: If you don't hear well . . .

KUMI MENSAH: I want to hear that from him. I want to hear him say that himself!

AWO: Well . . . Kwadwo, your father wants you to speak. Speak!

KUMI MENSAH: Yes, I'm listening! [*Pause*] Can't you speak?

KWADWO OKOTO: [*Prostrates himself before* KUMI MENSAH] Father, my mother is right. We are our father's children and by right of inheritance the heirs to our father's property. I and my brothers, excuse me putting it this way, are not stealing anything of yours. We are asking, merely asking, for what is due to us by right of inheritance.

KUMI MENSAH: You? You Kwadwo Okoto too? [*Calls*] Comfort! Comfort! Come here! Come here and listen to this! [*Laughs and moves towards* KWADWO OKOTO] Ungrateful! Ungrateful child! You were down on all fours begging me here only nine months ago. You dare come to me with that! Who taught you to think like that!

AWO: [*Laughing*] You look old, Kumi, but you're young . . . too young . . .

KUMI MENSAH: I am the head of the family. I am going to decide who should keep what of the family property.

AWO: We selected you to be the head of the family. And we have the power and the right to remove you . . . any time!

KUMI MENSAH: You? Remove me?

AWO: Listen, Kumi, listen and learn well! To be head of a family is not like 'Fufu'. It is like sacrifice! You serve, you don't command.

KUMI MENSAH: I have suffered on this land case for over seven years; wasted over 10,000 cedis . . . And on the very day that . . .

AWO: If you are honoured by people, don't dishonour yourself. We know you've spent a lot of money on this land case. Everybody knows this case has taken a lot out of your life. We know about all that. But why do you think we made you the head of the family? Our ancestors did more and complained even less.

KUMI MENSAH: I am not going to bear the burden of redeeming this land for your children.

KWADWO OKOTO: [*Bows*] Father . . . you are our head and our father . . .

KUMI MENSAH: Head! Father! Elder! With what do I become the head . . . with money? Power? Burdens? You . . . you Kwadwo . . . ungrateful! Shameless and ungrateful! You were ploughing at my feet begging me when you had your trouble with Alice . . . today, you dare come to me with . . . with . . . I fought for that farm for years! I fought alone! How . . . how dare you! You dare tell me today it is your property?

AWO: Is it your property?

KUMI MENSAH: Keep out of that! Just stay out of this case . . . You . . . you are the one inciting your children to . . .

AWO: I don't incite my own children. What concerns them concerns me too. And I have every right to fight for anything for them.

KWADWO OKOTO: [*Bows*] With all due respect, Father. I want you to understand that I and my brothers do highly appreciate all your past help. But you know yourself, THE PAST IS PAST. I think you will also agree with me that I have played the landless wandering subject of the family for too long. I am thirty-six, and now have a wife and a son; I must stand up and begin facing my own responsibilities now. And if I must be fully independent, then I must have the means to depend on my own self. We are therefore requesting you to give back to us what, by right of birth and of inheritance, is rightfully ours. So we can help our own selves to stand on our own feet.

AWO: [*Supporting* KWADWO OKOTO] If this reasonable demand doesn't strike him as simple and sensible, he can take us to court!

KUMI MENSAH: Court? Ha! You can't frighten a witch with red! I have been in court before and I can be there again.

KWADWO OKOTO: But you are my father and my protector. If you should stand against me in court, who should defend me?

AWO: He wants to divide the family, set man against man, son against father, that's all. We are all of the same blood, Kumi!

KUMI MENSAH: [*Calls*] Comfort! Comfort! God! I've been fighting all these years for nothing. Comfort!

AWO: Fonkorrt? Don't call a woman. Call on the gods themselves . . . to help you unite the family! That's what you must do! Because there is not going to be peace in this house any more, so long as you have what is mine . . . and my children's . . .

KUMI MENSAH: [*Sudden desperation*] Oh God! God! Gods of my fathers. Why? Why? Why? [*Muttering to self*] No . . . no more . . . no more . . .

The dog barks and yelps. A frightened sheep bleats and struggles. AUNTIE COMFORT *enters from the bedroom.* KUMI *tries to present his predicament to* COMFORT.

KUMI MENSAH: Comfort, listen to this . . .

COMFORT: Not now . . . not now . . . The sheep has ensnared itself . . .

KUMI MENSAH: Just listen to . . .

COMFORT: I must free the sheep . . . The dog's been frightening it since it was brought down . . .

KUMI MENSAH: Kwadwo and his mother, they want the land . . . our land . . .

COMFORT: You are the man, Kumi! I am only a woman!
[*Picks up a stone*] This foolish dog too . . . [COMFORT *crosses into the compound*]

Long pause. A loud howling from a wounded dog. KUMI MENSAH *collapses on the stool. Pause.*

KUMI MENSAH: Awo, I won't be the first head of a family to bring discord among people of the same house . . . of the same blood. You shall have your land . . .

AWO: You are now . . .

KWADWO OKOTO: Father . . .

KUMI MENSAH: Enough! Enough! [*Pause*] Kwadwo . . .

KWADWO OKOTO: Yes . . . Father . . .

KUMI MENSAH: You know the custom, as well as I do. A sheep must be slaughtered. Go . . . save for that. When you're ready, call the council of elders to witness the handing over. Your brothers must be there. I am not going to stand in the way of anybody trying to help himself. I should have helped my own children.

KWADWO OKOTO: [*Protesting*] Father . . .

KUMI MENSAH: Enough! [*Stands*] You want what you want! I lost it! You have it! There's nothing more to talk about! [*Pause*]

KWADWO OKOTO: [*Gets up*] Mother, help me thank my father.

Enter COMFORT *from the compound.*

AWO: We thank you, Kumi. We thank you in the name of all the seventy-seven gods of this land. Thank you, 'Ahenewa'.

KWADWO OKOTO: Thank you again, Father.

KUMI MENSAH: It's enough!

KWADWO OKOTO: Auntie Comfort, help me thank my father. He's just handed over the land to his children.

COMFORT: The cocoa farm?

AWO: Yes, the cocoa farm. He has given it to us.

KWADWO OKOTO: I told you this morning, there's been nothing but good luck signs and . . .

Speechless, COMFORT *looks at her husband for a moment.*

COMFORT: [*To* KUMI] They thank you.

KUMI MENSAH: Bring some whisky.

AWO: [*Gets up*] Ahhh . . . Kwadwo, if we have finished with your father . . . I must ask leave to go. I have to see about the child.

KWADWO OKOTO: I will come with you.

AWO: Stay here for a while and . . .

KWADWO OKOTO: I have to buy some towels for the child.

KUMI MENSAH: You are free to go. You both . . .

AWO: [*To* KWADWO OKOTO] You must come down with your brothers this evening and thank your father.

KWADWO OKOTO: I'll do that, Mama.

AWO: Eh! What did you say?

KWADWO OKOTO: [*Shouts*] I said, I will do that!

AWO: You must do more than that! From now on, you let me catch you once . . . just once more sitting under that mango tree playing draughts . . .

KWADWO OKOTO: Leave me alone! Why do you always want to pick on me in public like that for? Why? Why?

AWO: Shut up there and listen.

KWADWO OKOTO: I'm not a child any more, you understand! I'm not a child.

AWO: Know whom you're talking to! You hear me? Know whom you're talking to!

KWADWO OKOTO: You can go hang yourself!

AWO: . . . You heard him? You all heard him. He wants me to go hang myself.

KWADWO OKOTO: I'm tired! Tired!

AWO: If you had known what to do with your life, I wouldn't still . . .

KWADWO OKOTO: [*To* KUMI MENSAH] Father, excuse me! That old witch won't let me . . . [*He dashes out, swallowing his last word*]

Re-enter COMFORT *with a bottle of whisky.*

AWO: [*Complaining to* KUMI MENSAH] You heard him? You heard that. He called me a witch. He said I am an old witch . . .

KUMI MENSAH: [*Drinking*] Go! Go and settle that with him.

COMFORT: [*Consoling*] Don't kill yourself over him, Awo. The children of today are all alike. No respect. They simply are made to disrespect the elderly . . .

AWO: That's what I keep saying . . . The world is coming to an end! That's all there is to say. A few years ago, he would have slaughtered a whole sheep for that insolence . . . [*Pause*] Well . . . I have to go now. [*Pause*] I'm going now . . . [*She exits lonely*]

COMFORT: Well, Kumi, so you've given . . .

Re-enter AWO.

AWO: Oh . . . Fonkorrtee. I forgot. Do you have any tobacco? My snuff . . .

COMFORT: I'm sorry, Awo. Kumi smokes cigarettes now . . .

AWO: Selfishness! That's what I call it. Selfishness! How can one make snuff from a cigarette. These men never want an old woman to share anything of theirs with them. Cigarettes! [*Pause*] Well . . . I'm going! Hey Kumi, come down and see the child this evening. And you all get ready for the out-dooring. It's about time somebody named a child after you. Well . . . Yaa Asi, she's young woman now. The womb is hot. So think about it. [*Pause*] I'm going . . . [*She exits finally.* KUMI MENSAH *takes a swill*]

COMFORT: So. [*Pause*] So you've given the farm to Kwadwo and his brothers?

KUMI MENSAH: Comfort . . . let's not rub hot pepper into old sores . . .
    I'm tired now . . . I need some rest.

COMFORT: I asked you a question.

KUMI MENSAH: What is it? What do you want? I have nothing
    more . . .

COMFORT: Have you given the farm back to those lazy boys?

KUMI MENSAH: [*Struggling for the whisky*] It's their farm.

COMFORT: What do you mean it's their farm?

KUMI MENSAH: [*Pouring whisky*] It is their father's property.

COMFORT: So what? Their father's property, so what? You have your
    own children to provide for, you know that? Kwasi is going to
    school next year. Have you made any plans for his future?

KUMI MENSAH: Comfort . . . talk about something else. The farm is for
    Kwadwo and his brothers. It has always been.

COMFORT: It is your farm. And could be your children's too!

KUMI MENSAH: Have you finished?

COMFORT: [*Angered, through disappointment*] Kumi . . . if you're going to be
    so soft as to throw away a precious property just for a song . . . then,
    I'm also going to walk out of this house . . . just as simply as you threw
    away that farm.

KUMI MENSAH: You want to leave for your mother's again?

COMFORT: Just you wait and see.

KUMI MENSAH: Wait and see what?

COMFORT: Hand over the farm to them and you'll see what I mean.

KUMI MENSAH: [*Getting firm with* COMFORT] I'm about to have enough of
    you all. You can pack up! You can go away! I'm tired! Tired of it
    all!

COMFORT: Tired? And who isn't tired? I'm tired too; tired of waiting
    and hoping . . . tired of your sense of fair play to all . . .
    tired of your building mansions in the air. WHO TODAY,
    IN THIS WORLD, CARES MORE FOR THE
    WELFARE OF OTHERS THAN HIS OWN CHILDREN? I'm
    packing up this very evening! Wait! You'll see what I mean . . .
    [*Exits*]

KUMI MENSAH: [*Deeply emotional*] Ho! She can go away! Everybody can go
    away! [*Drinks*] Everybody can go anywhere they please! I have my
    own children. At least I'm their only father.

Enter COMFORT.

COMFORT: Give me the safe key.

KUMI MENSAH: So you're going away?

COMFORT: You give me the safe key.

KUMI MENSAH: Appeah will come back. He will . . .

COMFORT: I know. That's why I'm going away. Give me the key.

KUMI MENSAH: This is his house.

COMFORT: I know. I am leaving it for him. The safe key.

KUMI MENSAH: You're not leaving. Not when everything is going wrong like this . . .

COMFORT: You give me the safe key.

KUMI MENSAH: [*Last desperate attempt*] Sit down, Comfort. Sit down, for a few minutes. I'll tell you something. [COMFORT *remains standing*] Sit down. Just a few minutes. I want you to listen to this very important secret of my life. After that if you still want to go away, I won't hold you any more.

Pause.

COMFORT: [*Sits*] Only for a few minutes, mind.

KUMI MENSAH: Yaa Asi must listen to this too. [*Calls*] Yaa! [*Silence*] Yaa Asi! [*Long Silence*] Is Yaa Asi not in the room there?

COMFORT: [*Gets up and rushes to* YAA ASI*'s room*] She mustn't waste my time! If she's annoyed with herself . . . [*Opens door*] Yaa Asi! Kumi! Kumi! Come over here! Come see something!

KUMI MENSAH: What is it?

COMFORT: Yaa Asi!

KUMI MENSAH: What's happened to her? Anything . . .

COMFORT: The girl is . . .

KUMI MENSAH: She's what?

COMFORT: She's . . . She's GONE!

KUMI MENSAH: Dead?

COMFORT: She's run away! Her room . . . empty! Everything is gone!

KUMI MENSAH: God! God! God! Oh, no more . . . NO MORE!

COMFORT: She jumped through the back window! It's still left open.

Pause.

KUMI MENSAH: [*Gives a big sigh of a man who's hurt beyond belief*] Well . . . ? [*Drinks*]

COMFORT: She could not have gone far. You can still get her back home.

KUMI MENSAH: No! Let her go away. Let her go to wherever she wants to . . . [*Pause*] You can go wherever you want to go too. You all can go away. Appeah will come back one day. He will come back. [*Drinks and exits into his room*]

COMFORT: Drunk! What kind of man is this who can't stand on his own . . . well . . . It's not my fault . . . [*Enter* KUMI MENSAH. *He has a double-barrel gun*] Where are you going with that gun?

KUMI MENSAH: [*Loading gun*] The farm . . . visit the cocoa farm.

COMFORT: In your present state? [*Grabs gun from* KUMI] Give me that gun! If you want to shoot yourself, you wait until I am not in the house. I can't be a witness in any court.

A dog is heard barking.

KUMI MENSAH: Give me back my gun!

COMFORT: You're drunk!

KUMI MENSAH: Give me that gun! Give me that gun or I'll . . .

Dog barking. A heavy piece of metal is thrown at dog. Howling of wounded dog. Gate crashes open.

COMFORT: What's going on in you today?

KUMI MENSAH: Give me that gun!

COMFORT: [*Suddenly*] Kumi, we have a visitor! Here . . . go inside! Take the gun with you. [*Pushes* KUMI *into his room*]

Enter AUNTIE AYELE.

AUNTIE AYELE: Afternoon, Auntie.

COMFORT: Good afternoon.

AUNTIE AYELE: I want to see Appeah's father.

COMFORT: Please sit down.

AUNTIE AYELE: Thank you.

COMFORT: My husband is not very well today. Anything I can do for you?

AUNTIE AYELE: I was here this morning.

COMFORT: Yes. I was told you called.

AUNTIE AYELE: Are you Appeah's mother?

COMFORT: I am.

AUNTIE AYELE: Well . . . Simple and straight to the point. Your son Appeah lodged with me. He was miserable, no money, no shelter and he was hungry. I did all I could for him; fed him, gave him shelter and clothes . . . Then suddenly, one day, Appeah simply disappeared from my house. [*Shows her developing stomach*] And look what he's left me with!

COMFORT: I think this is too much for me. Let me get his father here . . . [COMFORT *crosses to bedroom door. She swings door open. With sudden horror . . .*] Stop him! He's put the gun to his head! Stop that, Kumi . . . STOP!

EXPLOSION! COMFORT *shrieks. Rushes to the baffled* AUNTIE AYELE.

COMFORT: Please . . . please help me.

AUNTIE AYELE: No . . . [AYELE *backing to exit*]

COMFORT: Please . . . help . . .

AUNTIE AYELE: No . . .

COMFORT: Help me . . .

AUNTIE AYELE: No . . .

COMFORT *pulls* AYELE *in.* AYELE *pulls herself to exit. The two women struggle each for herself. Sound of wounded dog in the background.*

Blackout.

CURTAIN

Blood and Tears

A Comedy of Assimilation

If the chameleon wants to burn, it is burnt.

Blood and Tears was first performed by the University of Ghana Drama Society at the University Drama Studio and at the 1973 Legon Festival of the Arts with the following cast:

CHARLES BROWN, *Robert Ansah*
ELSIE BROWN, *Philipa Dennis*
FLORA KOOMSON, *Patience Dowouna*
INSPECTOR COFIE, *Frank Dubley*
SERGEANT SMART, *V. G. D. Offei*

Characters

MR CHARLES ALLEN BROWN, *An electrical engineer*
MRS ELSIE BROWN, *His wife*
MISS FLORA KOOMSON, *Elsie's girl friend*
INSPECTOR COFIE, *Old and fat*
SERGEANT SMART, *Young and strong*

First Movement

The living room of Mr Charles Brown.

Three doors are seen.
Door left leads into the kitchen. Centre door into the bedroom. And right door to outside of the house and into town.

A very simple but well furnished living room.

Only a few items of furniture are seen but these are among the most modern on the market.

A beautiful bouquet of plastic flowers is on the stage centre coffee table. A writing desk and a bookshelf stand against the wall to stage centre and to stage left. A few books on engineering and sociology, the Complete Works of Shakespeare and the Complete Plays of Oscar Wilde are all neatly filed in the bookshelf.

A colour TV set stands downstage right.
A large record player is standing against the wall adjacent to TV set stage right. The floor is linoleum; well polished and very slippery.

Stage arrangement should not be symmetrically balanced.

A spotlight centre stage. Light searches from one end of stage to the other. Light stops dead centre stage, revealing a giant-size General Electric refrigerator standing against wall centre stage.

A kettle is heard whistling from the kitchen. The whistle grows louder and louder . . .

Enter ELSIE *from bedroom.*
ELSIE *is about thirty-five. She is expensively dressed in the latest women's wear on the fashion chart.*
She wears her hair straight and well-groomed. She is heavily made-up – to cover up her changing complexion. ELSIE *has* Woman's Wear Daily *in her left hand and a glass of Coca-cola in her right.*

ELSIE: [*Crossing into kitchen*] For heaven's sake! Can't a woman have a little peace of mind . . . [*Spills Coke on her dress*] Gracious! What a dirty thing! Spilled it all on me! [*Car horn from outside.* ELSIE *still brushing her dress*] Coming . . . God! The kettle . . . [ELSIE *crosses into kitchen*] [*Horn*] [ELSIE *from kitchen*] Heaven sake, Charles! What is it?

CHARLES: [*From outside*] I'm home. [*Horn*] Where are you?

ELSIE: Here!

CHARLES: Where?

ELSIE: In the kitchen. [*Kettle whistle goes off*]

CHARLES: [*Knocking at the door*] Open the door.

ELSIE: Can't you open it yourself?

CHARLES: I lost my key!

ELSIE: [*Enters from kitchen, still brushing dust from her dress*] Don't know where you keep your head sometimes . . .

Door right opens. Enter CHARLES. CHARLES BROWN *is a young man of about twenty-eight. Like* ELSIE, CHARLES *is expensively dressed, in a thick woollen suit and felt hat. He carries suit, an umbrella and a brief case.*

ELSIE: Lost your key almost every week . . .

CHARLES *leans on door frame and yawns.*

ELSIE: That yawn proves nothing. Look at your watch. Or did it stop working again?

CHARLES: [*With guilt*] The car. Trouble again . . . carburettor this time . . .

ELSIE: Car . . . carburettor . . . muffler . . . there's always something.

CHARLES: I do my best, Elsie!

ELSIE: Your best is not good enough, Charles. What you call your best is simply nothing . . .

CHARLES: Oh, my head . . .

ELSIE: If I look repulsive to you and you can't stand me any more . . . there . . . there is the door!

CHARLES: Okay . . . if you want . . . [CHARLES *turns, making for exit right*]

ELSIE: And where are you going?

CHARLES: Out.

ELSIE: Bye! Don't come to the house any more! Hear me? Don't come . . .

CHARLES: [*Angered*] I want to park my car. Just park my car. Am I allowed to?

ELSIE: You're not going out anywhere. You were a good two hours late coming home . . .

CHARLES *crosses to stage centre.*

CHARLES: [*Sits*] Okay . . . Okay . . . I'm two hours late . . . I'm sorry.

ELSIE: [*Sits*] I wasn't expecting you to say you weren't . . .

Long pause.

CHARLES: [*Trying to change the subject*] Darling . . .

ELSIE: What is it?

CHARLES: Is food ready? I am as hungry as a horse. [*Hits stomach*]

ELSIE: The repairman was here to fix the refrigerator. Took him a whole day adjusting one simple plug. Think he was fixing a king-pin set on the royal Rolls-Royce.

CHARLES: The fridge working again?

ELSIE: If it doesn't break down again tomorrow.

CHARLES: Wonderful! Terrific! I now can have my evening beer . . . [*Jumps up and attempts to embrace* ELSIE] Oh . . . you wonderful woman

ELSIE: [*Severely*] CHARLES!

CHARLES: Yes, Elsie darling . . .

ELSIE: Let go of me!

CHARLES: Uuuhh . . . darling . . . darling . . . be a little romantic.

ELSIE: [*Pushes* CHARLES *off violently*] Get away with you! You smell like petrol!

CHARLES: [*Disarmed, sniffs hand*] I do . . . I do . . . the car . . . carburettor . . . Well . . . eh . . . I'll clean up a bit . . . I'll wash my hands . . . [*Crosses to kitchen door. Crosses back*] Well . . . eh . . . [*Pause*] Can I have some beer?

ELSIE: You know the rule.

CHARLES: [*Crosses to fridge*] Okay . . . Okay . . . go finish with the cooking

ELSIE: Charles!

CHARLES: Yes. [CHARLES *confusedly turns again to refrigerator*]

ELSIE: Leave the fridge alone!

CHARLES: Just want to find out if it is working well.

ELSIE: Don't try any trick. The fridge is fine . . . I'm expecting a guest thi' evening . . .

CHARLES: I only wanted to check up . . .

ELSIE: Check up . . . supervise; that's all you know about. An electrical engineer who can't fix a plug. You . . .

CHARLES: It's okay! No beer, okay . . . but . . . but . . . Why do you always want to disgrace . . . I'm going out. [*Half way to door right*] I'm going to park the car in the garage.

ELSIE: You've all along been looking for some excuse to get out of the house anyway. Go! Go ahead! Spend the rest of the day parking that car. I'll do the cooking! [*Exit* ELSIE *into the kitchen*]

CHARLES: [*Pause*] Back home; back hell! [*Drinks left-over coke*] [CHARLES *at door right*] [*Knock from door right. No answer. Knock*]

ELSIE: [*From kitchen*] Will you please find out who's knocking, Charles?

CHARLES: Yes, dear . . .

CHARLES *opens door right.* FLORA KOOMSON, *a slim seductive woman of about twenty-five, is standing dead centre in the doorway. She smiles.* CHARLES *stares stock-still at* FLORA, *speechless.*

FLORA: [*Seductively*] Hello . . .

CHARLES: [*Calls*] Elsie! Elsie! It's a . . . girl! [*Spills coke on suit*] God! My suit! God! My suit!

FLORA: Does Mrs Brown live here?

CHARLES: Hello. [*Calls*] Elsie, she wants to . . . [*Pause, looks at* FLORA] Yes . . . she lives here. [*Calls*] Elsie, you have a visitor.

ELSIE: [*From kitchen*] Coming . . .

CHARLES *and* FLORA *stare at each other.*

FLORA: Well . . . can I come in?

CHARLES: Hmm?

ELSIE: [*Enters from kitchen*] Flora . . . it's Flora, darling! Dearest . . . Oh . . . you look even prettier than ever. Come in. Come right in. Sit here. . . . Charles, you should have let Flora in . . .

CHARLES: [*Still confused*] Right! Right! In a moment. I'll park my car now. [*Charles slips out*]

ELSIE: Oh . . . how are you, Flora? Please, sit down. Here . . .

FLORA: [*Standing*] Thank you.

ELSIE: Meet Charles . . . my husband . . . Charles? Charles? Where is that man?

FLORA: [*Sing-song*] He went out . . . that way.

ELSIE: Oh well . . . you met him anyway, didn't you?

FLORA: He seems familiar . . . but I don't think we really met. I saw your wedding picture in the *Sunday Mirror* though.

ELSIE: Those horrible pictures! I know! London may have the best of everything but it certainly has the worst photographers in the world.

FLORA: You both looked simply charming.

ELSIE: Well . . . not any more . . . with this six months saddle bag . . . [*Laughs*] Oh . . . please don't let me keep you standing. Make yourself comfortable!

FLORA: Well . . . I . . . [*Pause*]

ELSIE: Well? What is it, Flora? Please feel free, Flora, to . . .

FLORA: Well . . . eh . . . your sitting room. Like a palace . . .

ELSIE: Don't make fun of me.

FLORA: I'm not making fun of you. This is . . . it is the most dreamy . . . I mean the best furnished sitting room I have ever stepped into for years. I mean it. I really do.

ELSIE: Dear, you should have seen our apartment in London then. Don't let me keep you standing. Please sit down . . . Sit down . . .

FLORA: Well . . . If you insist. [*Pause*] But this faded dress on such beautiful cushions . . .

ELSIE: You look pretty in any dress, Flora. For a woman, the figure is what counts . . . and you have what Oscar Wilde describes as the 'true personification of the absolute perfect figure'. I do envy you. Every girl should!

FLORA: [*Springs in the chair*] Ooooohhhhh . . .

ELSIE: What is it, Flora?

FLORA: The chair . . . [*Springs*]

ELSIE: What?

FLORA: It's foamy . . . [*Springs*]

ELSIE: Mean comfortable?

FLORA: Very! You are a lucky woman. Elsie. Where did you . . . [*Spies around*] meet him?

ELSIE: In London.

FLORA: I wish I could go to London too. The men one meets around here these days . . . plain hopeless; just plain hopeless!

ELSIE: I'll get you some cool drinking water. Then you can tell me all that you've been doing with yourself since we last met.

FLORA: Nothing exciting ever happens in my life, Elsie. I've just been floating and wishing and hoping from day to day, that's all . . . well . . . I guess I can't change the world.

ELSIE: Get married, Flora.

FLORA: Get married?

ELSIE: A woman gets married. What else?

FLORA: I guess no one man was made for me. Elsie, somebody must give me the facts about these mysterious devils called the male sex. I simply don't get along well with them. Can't keep them after I got them. [*Sighs*] I am public property, now . . . Elsie; literally.

ELSIE: Someone will show up by and by. Some few years ago, I would never have believed I was ever going to be proposed to . . . much less be so happily married. But then . . . well . . . we women don't control the men there . . . Here's water.

FLORA: Thank you. [*Drinks*] Ohhh . . . ohhh . . .

ELSIE: What is it?

FLORA: My tooth.

ELSIE: Toothache?

FLORA: No . . . frozen . . .

ELSIE: Flora! No!

FLORA: The water . . . freezing cold! I know why. You have such a big refrigerator.

ELSIE: Well . . . one can't do any good housekeeping these days without a refrigerator, you know. [*Opens refrigerator*] Some beer?

FLORA: Doesn't hurt.

ELSIE: Local or imported? We prefer everything imported.

Enter CHARLES. *Stops in doorway.*

ELSIE: Ah . . . here now is the runaway husband. Flora, meet my husband, Charles Brown. Charles is the city electrical engineer, you know!

FLORA: Hello. [*Stretches out her hand.* CHARLES *still standing stock-still*]

ELSIE: Come down here and meet our guest, Charles.

CHARLES: I smell of petrol.

ELSIE: Don't be silly! Come over here and . . . [*Whistle from kitchen*] Oh . . . Oh . . . Oh . . . the rice! My rice! I hope it isn't . . . [*Rushes into kitchen*]

CHARLES: [*Walks to* FLORA] How do you do, Miss . . .

FLORA: Pretty fine, doing quite well. Thank you very many much . . . No . . .

CHARLES: Anything wrong?

FLORA: My language.

CHARLES: You're doing quite fine.

FLORA: You're teasing . . . Well . . . I never was in London.

CHARLES: You look as enlightened as my lady I met . . .

FLORA: Thank you. [*Enter* ELSIE]

ELSIE: Bless me. The rice is okay. Get some beer, Charles. Some beer for Flora.

CHARLES: Yes, dear . . . some beer . . . some . . . [*Running helter skelter*] [*Foolishly*] Some beer . . . some beer. Where is some beer?

ELSIE: You aren't funny, Charles. Flora, you have to excuse me for a few minutes. I have to finish with my cooking . . . Charles, here is a pearl sitting next to you but talk to . . . don't touch!

CHARLES: Like you say! [*Exit* ELSIE] Well . . . here is something cold for you. And mine! [FLORA *about to drink*] Wait a minute. Here . . . [*Clinks glasses*] Now then . . .

FLORA: My etiquette!

CHARLES: You're fine.

FLORA: Well . . . I never was in London.

CHARLES: Well . . . London . . . London . . . my second home.

FLORA: I remember about ten years ago, when Elsie was leaving the country. Oh, how I wished I were in her shoes. To see places like the London railway station, Buckingham Palace . . . a country and the beautiful places that we read about in school textbooks . . .

CHARLES: I know . . . I know . . . London City is a dream city. It's good to travel. See other strange lands and their different people and developments. The marvels of engineering and technology . . . London Bridge . . . Civilization! . . . The irresistible force that's transferred beer from barrels into bottles! All an eye to see . . .

FLORA: All far . . . far like a distant dream. We're late here.

CHARLES: Will never catch up. [*Pause*] What did you say your name is?

FLORA: Flora. Miss Flora Koomson.

CHARLES: Koomson . . . Koomson . . . that name rings a bell!

FLORA: Koomson? Rings like a bell?

CHARLES: I mean . . . [*Pause*] Yes . . . your name rings like a bell. Like this [*Strikes the drinking glass*] ding . . . dong . . . ding . . . dong . . . [*Forces a laugh*] Funny. Isn't it?

FLORA: A little. [CHARLES *drinks. Pause*]

CHARLES: You know something. I like your name. I really do. It's a very beautiful name. Poetic. Like . . . [*Pause*] Like Flora . . . sounds like Flurries . . . Flowers . . . Flowing . . . smooth and calm like clear mountain spring water. Or Flora . . . like flowers! Beautiful and blooming; with birds, bees and butterflies jumping from flower to flower; sucking from petal to petal; spreading nature's beauty and adding to love and life. I used to be romantic.

FLORA: London, they say, is the most romantic city in the world.

CHARLES: Paris. But London, that's the place for me. London, my second home. [*Pause*] Can I call you Flo?

FLORA: If your wife won't mind.

CHARLES: Tell me, Flo. Why is it that every girl who attended Achimota Secondary School is beautiful?

FLORA: Am I beautiful?

CHARLES: Pretty! Pretty is the word. [CHARLES *drains glass*] Let's have something really kicking, something really hot! Whisky?

FLORA: Fine.

CHARLES: There used to be a day when the palmwine was king! Then along came Scotch and out went that witch's brew . . . [*Reading label*] Blended by the master brains of the Scottish blend masters. By appointment to His Majesty King George VI himself. None, none but the best. [*Serving*] Soda?

FLORA: Dry.

CHARLES: Beautiful! Beautiful! That's how we drank whisky when we were in London. Your glass. Mine! [*Clinks*]. To my secret love . . .

FLORA: If I get senselessly drunk. . . . [*Sips*] That's good whisky.

CHARLES: I can't stand much whisky these days. [*Holds on to Flora*] Makes me nervous sometimes . . . How long have you been in the city?

FLORA: Five years.

CHARLES: Strange. And all along I thought I had seen all there is to see in the city.

FLORA: Haven't you?

CHARLES: No. You, for example . . .

FLORA: Me? [*Laughs*] Well, married men! You're not supposed to steal a look at other women when you drive past them, you know. [*Pause*] Elsie coming?

CHARLES: She's cooking . . .

ELSIE: [*From the kitchen*] Charles!

CHARLES: [*To* FLORA] Drink your whisky.

ELSIE: Charles!

CHARLES: Yes, honey . . .

ELSIE: How are you getting on with our guest?

CHARLES: Fine, Fine. Very fine. [*Pause, nervously to* FLORA] That's my wife. She does her best.

FLORA: She sure should. Aside of you, I don't think there are more than two more gentlemen living in the world today.

CHARLES: You women seem to spend most part of your day perfecting how to tie a man down. Always some sly soothing words; some articulate, perfectly structured, sweet-sounding phrases . . . but . . . like they say 'wait until the honeymoon is over'.

FLORA: It's always the woman. Men are ever such perfect . . . so perfect the good holy angels seem the sinners.

CHARLES: Please . . . don't get me wrong. I'm no angel. I'm only speaking like a practical husband who knows what he's talking about.

FLORA: At least, you sound sincere. [*A little drunk*] You're nice too. Very nice . . .

CHARLES: Please . . .

FLORA: I mean it. You're very nice. And you have everything in life to make a woman happy . . .

CHARLES: Everything in life?

FLORA: Yes. You have been to England; you are well educated; you have your own house; a car; a big refrigerator; a colour television set. What more? Can I have some more whisky?

CHARLES: Okay do! [CHARLES, *a little drunk*] [*Pouring whisky*] When I was in London, there were three of us . . . the three jungle jims [*Laughs*] by holy Jesus . . . we could gulp the stuff. [*With pride*] Drank whisky in mugs! Pure Scotch . . . not the watery stuff one drinks around here. [*Sighs*] Well . . . well, life will never be the same! I'll put on some records. [*Selecting an album*] Do you dance?

FLORA: Fairly. Do you?

CHARLES: God! I can wheel like Chaplin [*Demonstrating*] [CHARLES *puts on record. Music playing*] [*Like a Shakespearian actor*] May the kind lady do this dance with me.

FLORA: Dance?

CHARLES: [*As if drunk. Using a little force*] Come on . . .

FLORA: Your wife is in the house!

CHARLES: When I meet a pretty girl, I dance. [*Pulling* FLORA *with force*]

Come on! Let's dance ... [CHARLES *stops. Straightens tie, with all formality*] [*Courteously*] May I have this dance ... please, lady?

FLORA: Mr Charles ... I am a guest of your wife, who's been a very good friend of mine.

CHARLES: My wife's friend is my friend! Now let's dance.

FLORA: No ... No ... Can't ...

CHARLES: Don't waste good music. Come on ... be a lady ... A lady who refuses a gentleman a dance ...

FLORA: Okay ... if you want me to ... but ...

CHARLES *embraces* FLORA *violently. They dance close to each other,* CHARLES *whistling into* FLORA's *ear all along.*

CHARLES: You dance beautifully ...

FLORA: Thank you. [*He steps on her foot*] Easy!

CHARLES: Sorry ... [*They dance*] Know what? One of these days, I'm taking a pretty girl like you to one of the tip-top dances at the Hilton ...

FLORA: You're a married man you know.

CHARLES: Don't worry about my wife. I know how to handle her ... Good! Very good. Wonderful!

FLORA: [*Stops dancing*] What is it?

CHARLES: Excellent! My wife is on maternity leave from next month. I can talk her into leaving for her mother's ... and then ... [*Pause.* FLORA *crosses stage*] What is it?

FLORA: Nothing.

CHARLES: You sure? [FLORA *looks around the room. She is pleased by its material comfort*] What's wrong, Flo?

FLORA: Can I have a cigarette?

CHARLES: Sure ... anything.

CHARLES *produces a packet of imported cigarettes. He goes close to* FLORA, *to light the cigarette.* CHARLES *and* FLORA *very close to each other.* FLORA *does not take the cigarette, instead she puts her hand on* CHARLES' *shoulders. Only the music is heard, louder and louder, filling the whole room.*
Enter ELSIE *from the kitchen.* FLORA *and* CHARLES *break from each other.*

CHARLES: Flo ... Flow ... Flowing rice. How I long to have you in my dirty stomach ...

ELSIE: You food poets ... just set the table for me.

FLORA: Elsie, I must be on my way.

ELSIE: Not on my blessed rice ... you're having dinner with us.

CHARLES: I second ...

FLORA: It's late ...

CHARLES: I'll drive you back.

ELSIE: Yes, Charles will drive you back home.

FLORA: Well then . . .

CHARLES: Shall we all sit down?

They all sit at table with CHARLES *facing* FLORA.

Blackout.

Music very loud.

END OF FIRST MOVEMENT

Second Movement

As before, but fresh flowers replace plastic flowers.

FLORA: Charles, dear, you're home early today.

CHARLES: A man just drove off. Who was he?

FLORA: My uncle.

CHARLES: Uncle? You have an uncle in this city?

FLORA: Surprised?

CHARLES: You never mentioned any uncle . . .

FLORA: You never asked me . . . [CHARLES *rushes away from* FLORA. *Crosses to stage left*] CHARLES!

CHARLES: What is it?

FLORA: Shhh . . . don't move!

CHARLES: What?

FLORA: Stand still . . . still . . . stiff . . . stiffer . . . don't even breathe . . . [FLORA *removes strand from* CHARLES' *hair*] Here! Cobweb!

CHARLES: That's all?

FLORA: [*Runs her hand through* CHARLES' *hair*] Keep it spotless clean for a dear one.

CHARLES: [*Totally overwhelmed. Hugging her*] Oh . . . Flora . . . You're so . . . so . . .

FLORA: You're squeezing me . . .

CHARLES: You smell good.

FLORA: The fresh flowers. [*Completely meshed up in each other for a while*] Charles . . .

CHARLES: Uuuuuuuuuuuhhhmmmmmmmmmmmmm . . .

FLORA: You aren't a jealous man, are you?

CHARLES: Nooo . . .

FLORA: That's sweet of you . . . [*Disengages*] I'll get you some beer . . .

CHARLES: [*Sees the flowers*] My! You're really doing such wonders to the house. Look at all the fresh flowers. You've certainly brought back life into this dead house. You know what? You have also charmed me with your beauty and . . .

FLORA: Please, Charles.

CHARLES: I'm not bragging. You're the prettiest, the most charming . . . and . . . and . . . girl I've ever met.

FLORA: I bet you have been saying the same things to a thousand and one girls, Charles.

CHARLES: Never! You are the only one . . .

FLORA: What about your wife?

CHARLES: Do you have to remind me every morning, noon and night that I am a married man?

FLORA: But you are married, aren't you?

CHARLES: I know that!

FLORA: Oh, poor dear. Poor, poor dear . . . Don't be annoyed with a silly girl like me. Come, show me a little sweet smile. You look ugly when you're annoyed. Smile . . . [CHARLES *smiles*] That's better. Now, I promise you, [*Scout salute*] on my honour, I'll never mention your wife again; in day or night; in rain or shine; so help me Charles!

CHARLES: [*Pleased with the show*] You . . . you're such a wonderful . . . wonderful woman!

FLORA: Here! Let me help you take off your coat and tie.

CHARLES: A kiss . . .

FLORA: Here. [*Kisses him*]

CHARLES: Wonderful! Wonderful! You know everybody in the office is beginning to notice that I'm putting on weight recently.

FLORA: I'll get you some cold . . . cool . . . beer.

CHARLES: I forgot all about it. I drank the last bottle of beer yesterday.

FLORA: I can be a good wife, you know. Everything is well straightened out! There are now twice as many bottles of beer in the house as we had yesterday. But the whisky . . . there was only a bottle left from yesterday but my Uncle Frank drank it.

CHARLES: I'll buy some more whisky tomorrow.

FLORA: [*Serves beer*] Here you are. [*Sing-song*] Drink and be merry, drink and be merry . . . I'll get you your food.

CHARLES: Is food ready?

FLORA: Hours ago. Oh, some music! [*Puts on music*] Now you can relax and remember all those sweet dreams.

CHARLES: My favourite number! Flora . . .

FLORA: Yes.

CHARLES: Let's dance.

FLORA: Never dance on an empty stomach.

CHARLES: Come on now, just one dance.

FLORA: I'll bring your food. [*Exit* FLORA *swinging her hips in time to the music*]

CHARLES: [*Overcome*] God! That woman will kill me! [CHARLES *whistles to the tune and dances alone*]

FLORA: [*Enters with food*] You sure are happy today.

CHARLES: [*Singing*] Dance a little dance with me sweet darling. [CHARLES *tries to embrace* FLORA]

FLORA: Charles! The food! You'll knock the whole thing over!

CHARLES: [*Opens cover and smells food*] Uuhhmmm . . . smells good . . .

FLORA: You really are happy today. Somebody must have shown you some big money in the office.

CHARLES: Sit here. Sit right here while I blow my chops! You'll give me extra appetite. [*Like a Shakespearian actor*] You, O! You, sweet appetizing beauty. Sit thou by my right that I might eat thy sweet food cooked by thy golden hand. [*Kisses her hand*]

FLORA: What's got into you this evening?

CHARLES: [*Shakespearian*] Sweet Flora, in thy name I eat. [*Bites*] Oh, I nearly forget all about it! The estate manager was in my office this morning. I think I can buy you the house, after all.

FLORA: The money . . .

CHARLES: Let the bank worry about that!

FLORA: Ten thousand, five hundred . . .

CHARLES: Good things cost more . . .

FLORA: Charles, you can at least ask the estate manager to knock the price down a bit. One buys furniture after . . .

CHARLES: Furniture? Fickle! I can handle that. A few hundred cedis, that's all. But no colour TV for you, that's for sure.

FLORA: What about my wrist watch, Charles? You promised me a watch.

CHARLES: Next week. Friday. Friday, payday!
  [*Sings*] Saturday you no come to me;
        Monday you no come to me;
        Every day you no come to me;
        Friday, na payday, you come to me.
  Ha, ha, ha, ha!

FLORA: You are spending too much money on this house.

CHARLES: Nonsense!
  [*Sings*] Your house is my house.
        We'll share the future together.

FLORA: You don't understand. What I'm trying to say is . . . I've been thinking . . . can't we share this house together? You . . . me and Elsie?

CHARLES: How?

FLORA: Well . . . I mean everybody knows I've been living here with you since your wife left.

CHARLES: Yes . . . but . . . but . . . I'm a married man.

FLORA: You want to be reminded of that, eh?

CHARLES: Well . . . I mean . . .

FLORA: Forget it!

CHARLES: I don't mean to . . .

FLORA: Eat!

CHARLES: What I mean is . . . I didn't mean to offend you.

FLORA: Why should I be offended? Eat! Tomorrow morning, we will go and see about the house.

CHARLES: Tomorrow. Yes, first thing tomorrow morning. And I'm going to buy you the best furniture ever to furnish a pretty lady's flat. That's a promise!

FLORA: Eat!

CHARLES: Agreed then? Tomorrow, first stop, the broker's office. Then my love's house here I come. [*Laughs*]. [*Pause*]

FLORA: Charles . . .

CHARLES: Sweety . . .

FLORA: You promised me a new 'Kente' cloth . . .

CHARLES: I did. I did. Next week. Remind me about it next weekend.

FLORA: Oh . . . I almost forgot. There's a dance tonight at the Star Hotel.

CHARLES: You want to go to the dance?

FLORA: If you want to.

CHARLES: I like Meridian Hilton dances better. I thought you said last week we were going to go to Meridian roof-top.

FLORA: My evening dress.

CHARLES: What's wrong with your evening dress?

FLORA: I can't wear the same dress twice to the same place.

CHARLES: What's wrong with wearing the same dress twice to the same . . .

FLORA: Charles, you're not a woman. You don't understand.

CHARLES: All I know is I've been wearing the same suit to the place for a whole year. Okay. We will go to the Star Hotel dance tonight. Tomorrow I shall see what I can do about a new evening dress for you. Then . . . ha . . . ha . . . ha . . . Meridian Hilton here I come. [*Singing and waltzing*] Dancing with my darling . . .

FLORA: You haven't touched your food.

CHARLES: [*Singing*] To the Tennessee Waltz,
                        When an old friend . . .

FLORA: There's something wrong with you . . .

CHARLES: [*Singing*] That I happen to know . . .

Tune from the music Tennessee Waltz takes over.

Lights fade down slowly.

END OF SECOND MOVEMENT

Third Movement

Music time is over. A large-size baby cot stands in place of the record player against the wall stage right. Fresh flowers replaced by plastic ones.
CHARLES, *half drunk, knocks on door right.*

ELSIE: Coming . . .

Pause. Hard knock.

ELSIE: What's got into you, Charles? The child is sleeping.
CHARLES: Come on! Open the door. [ELSIE *opens door,* CHARLES *walks in*] Who asked you to lock the door?
ELSIE: It's half past nine!
CHARLES: So what?
ELSIE: You left the office at five. Where have you been?
CHARLES: Anything you want me to do in the house for you?
ELSIE: You know the child hasn't been well since yesterday.
CHARLES: Take him to the doctor!
ELSIE: You can at least come home and . . .
CHARLES: Is that one child too much of a burden on you, already . . . ?
ELSIE: I think it is about time somebody straightened you up! What kind of father are you anyway? How do you expect me to maintain a decent family in this house when you, the father of my child, can . . .
CHARLES: Elsie . . . I'm tired . . .
ELSIE: Of who? Me or your son?
CHARLES: Of this very damn house! Of your cackling! Of everything! Why don't you leave me alone? Why . . .
ELSIE: Like you leave me alone?
CHARLES: Where's my newspaper? I better read. [*Hides behind newspaper*]
ELSIE: You're not hiding your guilt behind any newspaper. You're telling me where you've been since you left the office. I am your wife, and demand to know everything . . .
CHARLES: I am not a boy . . . a child . . . I am a full grown man. And if . . .
ELSIE: If you're not going to behave yourself like a grown up man, I'm going to check and straighten you up like a boy! I'm the mother of your son . . .
CHARLES: Mother of my son . . . so what, Elsie? So what? So what do you want me to do? Jump over the sea? Or keep data, a log book about my movements and gestures and my . . . my activities . . .

ELSIE: If it's necessary to keep a log book, yes! You're going to! Especially now when your movements and activities are getting more and more shady and suspicious . . .

CHARLES: Okay, settled! Buy me the log book and I'll keep the record straight for you. Satisfied?

ELSIE: You can do whatever you like. Can even ask for divorce if . . .

CHARLES: Okay, okay . . . now give me something to eat.

ELSIE: There is no food in the house.

CHARLES: There is no what? [*Pause*] Come on, say that again. I don't think I heard you properly. There is no *what* in the house?

ELSIE: You haven't been eating in this house for more than three days. I can't waste time and food when you . . .

CHARLES: [*Outburst*] God! Listen to her! Listen to the all knowing, the modern mother . . . the civilized wife! No food in the house! Just like that! Blunt, shameless and as simple an explanation as that from the woman I married with my money!

ELSIE: Charles . . . it's not my fault.

CHARLES: Of course, it's never been your fault. It's been my fault all along. I decided to get married! The hell I did! [*Opens refrigerator*] Where is the beer I left here in the fridge?

ELSIE: I don't drink beer.

CHARLES: [*Shouting*] Where's the beer? That's my question. Answer it! And stop quoting me facts and statistics about some sickening self chastity. Every woman is pure!

ELSIE: Just what does that mean?

CHARLES: It means 'Who drank those beers?'

ELSIE: Somebody . . . a man came down this evening . . .

CHARLES: Just as I thought. One of those mysterious uncles of yours, who pop out from nowhere and always escape through the bedroom window.

ELSIE: What's got into you tonight, Charles?

CHARLES: I'm cracked up! Mad! Mad as a hare!

ELSIE: You really look like you need the doctor . . .

CHARLES: And a lawyer . . . and a private detective . . . maybe then one can find out if there still is a faithful woman living under this sun.

ELSIE: If you're through whoring around with your thousand and one girl friends . . . keep it to yourself. Don't hide your guilt behind some feeble imagination that I do the silly things you've been doing in the dark . . . It was your goldsmith who . . .

CHARLES: Who?

ELSIE: Your goldsmith.

CHARLES: I don't know any goldsmith.

ELSIE: I don't expect you to admit you know any goldsmith.

CHARLES: I don't know any goldsmith.

ELSIE: The man you bought the gold necklace from.

CHARLES: I don't know what you're talking about.

ELSIE: [*Turns to attack*] Did you buy any gold necklace for me, Charles?

CHARLES: Look . . . Elsie, I'm tired and hungry . . .

ELSIE: [*Very serious*] Charles . . . a man, a strange man was in this house this evening to collect his money from you. That man said you, Charles, bought a gold necklace from him . . . for your wife . . . Did you buy any gold necklace from anybody?

CHARLES: What if I did?

ELSIE: [*Firmly*] Did you buy any necklace?

CHARLES: Yes, I did.

ELSIE: Where is it?

CHARLES: Where is what?

ELSIE: The necklace! Don't play dumb! Where is it!

CHARLES: It wasn't exactly a gold necklace . . .

ELSIE: What exactly was it?

CHARLES: Just a plain necklace . . . not gold.

ELSIE: And you bought that plain necklace for your wife?

CHARLES: I bought . . . Look, Elsie . . . let's forget about the whole thing. I'm hungry.

ELSIE: Charles, you bought a necklace costing five hundred and fifty cedis.

CHARLES: [*Show of force*] What do you want of me, Elsie? What do you want of my life? You want me to draw a balance sheet of it, so you can check and balance it. Tell me, what do you want? I'm not a child still! I'm not!

ELSIE: [*In anger*] And I'm not the docile, the silly, stupid, credulous, good, Bible-obedient kind of wife you take me for! You are telling me everything about that mysterious necklace here and now . . . or, my God, one of us will . . .

CHARLES: The child is sleeping.

ELSIE: I don't care if he's crying. You're telling me . . .

CHARLES: Okay . . . Okay . . . if you want to know I'll tell you. I wanted to tell you about it all along . . . but . . . but . . . I thought . . . [*Pause*]

ELSIE: Yes, you thought what?

CHARLES: I'm trying to explain!

ELSIE: I'm listening. Go on.

CHARLES: Well . . . eh . . . I . . . bought a necklace [*Pause*] I bought a necklace . . . for you . . . as a present . . . after you delivered . . . but . . . I don't know what happened. I think I got drunk somewhere. And lost it . . . I don't know where.

ELSIE: [*With pity*] I pity you . . . Have you convinced yourself with that explanation of yours?

CHARLES: That's the truth . . .

ELSIE: It is true also that I don't seem to know what you've been doing with your money these days. Don't imagine I walk around with my two eyes closed . . .

CHARLES: You know, the car . . . spare parts . . . petrol . . . workshop . . . expenses . . .

ELSIE: Don't draw me a balance sheet on your private life. I'm not interested.

Knock at door right. CHARLES *and* ELSIE *look at each other. Pause. Louder knock.*

CHARLES: [*Helplessly*] Are you expecting anybody?

ELSIE: No. Are you? [*Knock*] Your goldsmith is back.

CHARLES: Who?

ELSIE: Your goldsmith. Answer the door! [*Charles hesitates. Knock*] Answer the door!

CHARLES: I will . . . I will . . . [*Hesitates for a moment. Opens door right.* FLORA KOOMSON *is standing centre blocking the doorway*] [*Confused*] Oh . . . eh . . .

ELSIE: Flora! Dear Flora! Darling! It's you! Charles, don't stand there staring at Flora as if she is some total stranger. Don't you recognize her?

CHARLES: [*Walks away*] . . . I recognize her.

ELSIE: [*Knocks* CHARLES *lightly on the head*] Oh, Charles, when you're hungry, you behave like some . . .

FLORA: Good evening, Mrs Brown.

ELSIE: Well, Flora, what style!

FLORA: Good evening, Mr Brown.

CHARLES: Thank you. How are you?

ELSIE: Flora, I love your skirt. It's so beautiful. Where did you buy it?

FLORA: I made it myself.

ELSIE: Oh, it is so beautiful. The pleats . . . so lovely! Please, sit down.

FLORA: Thank you. [*Sits*]

ELSIE: You deserve a big knock on the head, Flora. Why is it that you haven't been to see us since I got back from maternity leave? Nearly six months now, isn't it, Charles?

CHARLES: Six months . . .

FLORA: I'm sorry, Elsie. I haven't been very well lately. How are you and Charles getting along?

ELSIE: [*Holds* CHARLES' *hand*] Just wonderful. Charles has always been such a darling. Aren't you Charles?

CHARLES: Wonderful . . .

FLORA: You always have had all the luck, Elsie. I met a very nice young man when you were away on maternity leave. For a while, I thought he loved me . . . but then . . . well . . . easy come, easy go.

ELSIE: Have hope! You still have your perfect figure, someone will fall into your trap by and by . . . But don't forget, next time, bring the young man here. Maybe Charles and I can serve to convince him that it's always good to have a woman at home.

FLORA: I don't know . . .

ELSIE: You never can tell. These days one has to trick the men into getting married, you know.

FLORA: Elsie, I think your husband is not interested in our girlish gossip . . .

ELSIE: Him? That bug under bedsheets. I tell you he enjoys every minute of any popular gossip . . . you name it. Don't you, Charles?

CHARLES: Eh? Oh, yes, yes, I'm a married man alright. [*Anger*] You know about that, don't you?

ELSIE: Oh, I didn't know?

CHARLES: What do you mean, 'you didn't know'?

ELSIE: Come on . . . Charles, what's biting you?

CHARLES: Just don't want to be pointed at and picked on again and again as an example of the unfaithful husband. I have always been faithful to you, haven't I?

ELSIE: Charles, tell me, what's been going through your mind?

CHARLES: What do you mean by 'What's been going through my mind?' What else . . .

A baby crying in room leading off stage door centre.

CHARLES: The child is weeping! Can't you hear?

ELSIE: Oh . . . my little . . . little dolly. My little dolly is awake. I'll bring him in here. [*Exit* ELSIE]

CHARLES: [*In anger. Pounces on* FLORA] What do you want here? What are you trying to prove? You know Elsie is in the house! What do you want here?

FLORA: [*Cool but serious*] Charles, if you don't pay the electricity bill by tomorrow evening, my lights will be cut off!

CHARLES: I'll get the money tomorrow! I promised you that! Look, I have been to the money lender's house three times this evening.

FLORA: I'm not interested in your money lender. My lights . . .

CHARLES: Give me some time . . . just a little more time! Tomorrow morning . . .

FLORA: My lights are being cut off tomorrow.

CHARLES: Shhh! Quiet! She's coming.

Enter ELSIE *with a baby in her arms.*

ELSIE: Flora . . . there you are. Meet my beautiful . . . beautiful paapa!

FLORA: Well . . . what a sweet little thing! Oh . . . Elsie . . . I envy you, this time even more. [*Lightly*] Is child stealing allowed here?

ELSIE: Where my baby goes, I go. [*Whistle from kettle*] Oh, the kettle! Hold the baby for me. I have to steam up some food for my hungry Charles. This husband of mine, whenever he is hungry, his mind swims

FLORA: I'm not sure I'm staying around that long . . . I was just passing through . . .

ELSIE: It won't take a minute!

FLORA: Well . . . [*Takes child from* ELSIE. *Plays with child*] Ahhh . . . that's my baby. You're going to be my little leetle . . . hus-band.

ELSIE: He's all yours. [*Exit* ELSIE *into kitchen*]

FLORA: Don't be long. I must be going soon.

ELSIE: Be back soon.

Pause. CHARLES *and* FLORA *stare at each other.*

CHARLES: [*After a long pause*] I like the way you're holding the child. [*No answer from* FLORA. *A long pause*]

CHARLES: I like . . . I like the way . . .

FLORA: Well . . .

CHARLES: Well?

FLORA: The money, I am waiting.

CHARLES: I haven't any money on me right here.

FLORA: You asked for it, Charles, and you're going to have it really hot, like it is.

CHARLES: But . . . when I had money . . .

FLORA: I don't want to hear anything about the past. I am talking about the present now. And you're giving me the money now before I leave this house. Or . . . my God! Everything is going to blow up, right here, in front of everybody! Well . . .

CHARLES: [*After a short pause*] How much exactly do you want?

FLORA: I told you I'm running out of food, there is the light bill, and the house boy has not been paid for nearly two months.

CHARLES: Will fifty cedis be alright?

FLORA: For the light bill?

CHARLES: I'll find out what I can do to raise some more money tomorrow. [*Pause*]

FLORA: Give me the fifty. [*Child weeps*]

CHARLES: Elsie . . . Elsie darling . . .

ELSIE: [*From the kitchen*] Yes, Charles. [*Enter* ELSIE] Oh . . . my baby . . . baby don't cry. Mother will be ready soon. [ELSIE *takes the baby*] [*Sings*] Baby little boy don't cry . . .
  Baby little boy don't cry . . .
  Mama is making you . . .

FLORA: I'm sorry, Elsie.

ELSIE: Nothing, Flora.

CHARLES: Elsie.

ELSIE: Yes, darling.

CHARLES: Do you have any loose money on you? Something, anything up to, say, fifty cedis?

ELSIE: What do you need money at this time of night for?

CHARLES: I want to pay my vulcanizer on the way when I drive Flora home.

ELSIE: It's late Charles. Nobody . . .

CHARLES: I'm sending the money to the house. He needs it badly. Understand the wife hasn't been well lately and . . .

ELSIE: Well . . . I'm not sure I have that much money on me . . . maybe thirty cedis . . . yes . . . but fifty . . .

CHARLES: Thirty will be fine.

ELSIE: Alright. I'll get it for you then. Can you hold the child for me again?

FLORA: Give him to me.

ELSIE: Very adorable. [*Gives child to* FLORA. *Exit* ELSIE *into bedroom. Child begins weeping*]

FLORA: Oh . . . baby . . . don't cry. Don't cry little bouncing . . . bonny . . .
[*Sings*]   Papa little boy don't cry . . .
Papa little boy don't cry . . .
Your Mom and Pap say . . .
Papa little boy don't cry . . .

CHARLES: You're doing great this time with the child. Look, he's smiling . . . you know, that's why I like you.

FLORA: That's why what?

CHARLES: I mean . . . I like you . . . I like you very much.

FLORA: I don't still wear a bib around my neck, Charles.

CHARLES: Flora . . . you see, you have to understand my position too. I'm trying to provide for you. I mean, you and my wife and child. I'm doing my best! Just that things are not the roses they used to be any more. You've got to understand . . . sympathize with my position a bit!

FLORA: You don't deserve any sympathy, Charles.

CHARLES: At least, give me a little more time. Tomorrow, trust me, tomorrow everything is going to be fine.

FLORA: How fine, Charles? Just how fine? Are you going to marry me tomorrow . . . or the day after tomorrow? Take a second wife?

CHARLES: [*Shocked*] Second wife? How?

FLORA: Simple. Just as you're keeping me as your mistress.

CHARLES: But . . . but . . . a second wife? But Flora, that's old fashioned . . . horrible . . . primitive . . . I'm educated . . . [*Enter* ELSIE]

ELSIE: Yeesss, everybody knows you are educated . . . you went to one of the best universities in London . . . but it's past midnight. You want to drive Flora home now? Here . . . the money [*Counting*] . . . twenty-eight, twenty-nine, thirty. Thirty cedis. And if you see the vulcanizer's wife, send my greetings and sympathy.

CHARLES: Thank you . . . I'll take you home now, Flora.

ELSIE: My baby . . .

As CHARLES *prepares to escort* FLORA *out, lights begin to dim slowly.*

FLORA: Here . . .
ELSIE: Charles, don't stay out too long. You haven't eaten this evening.
FLORA: Bye, Elsie.
ELSIE: Bye, Flora.
CHARLES: Be back soon.

Blackout.

END OF THIRD MOVEMENT

Fourth Movement

Stage is dark. Wall clock strikes twelve. CHARLES *enters from door right. He tiptoes stealthily into room.* ELSIE *switches on the light.*

CHARLES: Elsie! . . . You . . . you still awake? Why haven't you gone to bed?

ELSIE: [*Seriously*] What time is it now, Charles?

CHARLES: A little past midnight.

ELSIE: When did you leave the office today?

CHARLES: Why do you want to know?

ELSIE: [*In anger*] Because I demand to know!

CHARLES: Don't shout. It's late . . .

ELSIE: Where have you been?

CHARLES: Elsie, it's too late at night to rage and shout over nothing, nothing at all. Go to bed. We shall talk in the morning.

ELSIE: [*Grabs* CHARLES *by his flying tie*] We're settling everything tonight and right here! Don't take me for the fool you . . .

CHARLES: Take your hands off my tie! You want to choke me to death?

ELSIE: Where did you go?

CHARLES: You're killing me!

ELSIE: Die if you want! Where did you go?

CHARLES: Relax! Relax! I'll tell you . . .

ELSIE: Yes, tell me. [ELSIE *lets go of the tie*]

CHARLES: Ahh . . . my tie! You nearly choked me to death. [CHARLES *takes off his tie*]

ELSIE: Well . . . I'm listening . . .

CHARLES: [*Matter-of-factly*] You want to know? Okay . . . I visited some friends.

ELSIE: What friends?

CHARLES: My girl friends! Are you satisfied now?

ELSIE: At least, for once, you're being honest. Go on now . . . who's that girl?

CHARLES: What girl?

ELSIE: The girl you've been visiting! Don't play dumb!

CHARLES: God! Tell a woman any bloody lie and she takes it for a gospel truth! You believe that I went to meet a girl?

ELSIE: You think you're clever? You're anything but clever, Charles. You're caught red-handed this time! You're not going to tell the truth to cover any lie like you've always been doing. [*Produces a letter*] Who wrote this?

CHARLES: What's that?

ELSIE: Don't pretend. You received this only yesterday!

CHARLES: [*Crosses stage*] Elsie, it's late. I need some sleep.

ELSIE: [*Blocks his way into bedroom*] Don't try my temper, Charles! Don't try my temper . . . You . . .

CHARLES: But what do you want?

ELSIE: Who wrote this letter?

CHARLES: Out of the way! [*Anger*] I say out of my way! Out!

ELSIE: You can kill me! No wonder you even keep a gun on you these days.

CHARLES: Look, Elsie, don't provoke me!

ELSIE: You're not getting away with it, be you the devil or hell itself!

CHARLES: It's the middle of the night. The whole neighbourhood is sleeping.

ELSIE: We'll wake them up, I don't care! I'm going to expose everything about your shady life! I'll strip that myth of super-gentility, the shameless pretences! What kind of educated man are you?

CHARLES: I have to ask you the same question. What kind of woman are you?

ELSIE: Who is that girl? You're telling me who she is; what she is to you; how long you've been seeing her . . . You are telling me everything, or by God, you'll find out what I'm really made of!

CHARLES: Elsie, be a little reasonable! Everybody is sleeping . . . we're disturbing the whole neighbourhood .

ELSIE: We have disturbed nothing yet! We are going to pull this very house down this very evening. Don't mistake my past silence for a weakness! I can run you out of this house! And I can keep you out of it, forever! Who is that girl?

CHARLES: What are you doing! You'll rip my shirt to pieces . . .

ELSIE: Then we rip it to pieces! I'm not going to sit by, docile like your trained dog, while you misbehave yourself at will! Who is that girl? Flora Koomson, is it?

CHARLES: Ha! Don't know what you're saying.

ELSIE: Don't deny it? This is Flora's handwriting!

CHARLES: You can think what you like!

ELSIE: Yes! And I can do what I like to you too! Get out of my house!

CHARLES: This? Your house?

ELSIE: Out this minute! Out! [*Picks up flower pot. Plastic flowers in pot drop all over the floor. Chases* CHARLES *out using the flower pot as weapon*] Out! Out! of my sight! [CHARLES *rushes out.* ELSIE *slams door on him*] Never again! Ever!

CHARLES [*Banging*] I'll knock the house down!

ELSIE: Get away! Get away Charles!

CHARLES *banging*.

NEIGHBOURS: You're disturbing us!
We're sleeping!
Keep quiet there!
Noise! Noise!
Call the police!
Why can't you live in peace, you fools!
You fools, do you know what time it is?
ELSIE: Shut up, all you there. Shut up there! What do you all know about what I am going through?

Loud knock.

VOICE: Open the door there, Mrs Brown. This is the police.

Banging from CHARLES.

CHARLES: Elsie, open the door.
ELSIE: Never! Never!

Banging.

Blackout.

END OF FOURTH MOVEMENT

Fifth Movement

FLORA KOOMSON's *sitting room. Identically furnished except for the absence of a TV set. Background noise from radio.*

FLORA KOOMSON *enters from bedroom; she is followed closely by* SERGEANT SMART.

FLORA: What time is it, Sergeant?

SMART: Almost midnight . . . I must be leaving now.

FLORA: Keep me company for a few minutes.

SMART: I am on duty.

FLORA: Please.

SMART: Sorry . . .

FLORA: What will you drink? Whisky? Gin? Beer?

SMART: Now, Flora, don't . . .

FLORA: Please.

SMART: Well, beer then.

FLORA: [*Crosses to fridge*] Strong and warm-blooded men, like sergeants, certainly don't need hot drinks like whisky.

SMART: Not again.

FLORA: Why not? You are, to me, what I call 'the real man'! Now drink something cool and calm down for me.

SMART: You make me feel guilty. I've been drinking free beer in this house for almost three months. And you won't accept a pesewa from me.

FLORA: A woman should spend just a little for the man she really cares for . . .

SMART: A rich woman, yes; but what if you are as wretched as some girls . . .?

FLORA: Want money? I can loan you money in hundreds. And you don't have to pay back.

SMART: On top of all the gallons of beer? No thanks.

FLORA: Oh poor . . . poor . . . Charles.

SMART: My name is Smart. Not Charles.

FLORA: God! This slip of the tongue. It'll get me into trouble one day.

SMART: It's the third time this evening that . . .

FLORA: Please, drink your beer.

SMART: Who's this Charles?

FLORA: Which Charles?

SMART: Don't pretend!

FLORA: Pretend about what?

SMART: About that Charles. One's tongue can't slip on the same name three times in less than an hour.

FLORA: Fill your glass . . . or let me fill it for you.

SMART: Don't change the subject. [FLORA *suddenly laughs loud.* SMART *is confused*] What is it? What's going on? What's so funny?

FLORA: Look!

SMART: What?

FLORA: There.

SMART: Where?

FLORA: Down there.

SMART: Down where?

FLORA: Flap . . .

SMART: God! My zip! [*Zips up*]

FLORA: Brave boy . . .

SMART: Don't tease . . .

FLORA: Super Smart!

SMART: I just forgot to zip up, that's all! I must go now . . . [*Gulps*]

FLORA: Please keep me company for a while . . . I feel so troubled tonight and . . . and . . . so lonely.

SMART: Sorry, but I'm on duty.

FLORA: Oh, I've got to show you this . . . I bought a new record today. Current popular hit. Want to hear it?

SMART: Next time . . . Have whisky with me.

FLORA: I have three bottles. Want one? I can give you one. Inspector . . . [*Stops short*]

SMART: There is an inspector too, eh? I better be going now, I'm only a sergeant.

FLORA: Your beer . . .

SMART: No more . . .

FLORA: When will I see you again?

SMART: Don't know.

FLORA: Tomorrow?

SMART: Maybe.

FLORA: Come down in the morning . . . we can have breakfast together.

SMART: I can't come.

FLORA: Why, Sergeant? Why?

SMART: Look, Flora, we have known each other for the past three months. And three months is quite a long time to know a woman well enough to be frank about her. So let me be frank with you. You and I simply don't match . . .

FLORA: Don't match? How?

SMART: You are rich.

FLORA: [*Laughs*] Rich?

SMART: At least, you have been introduced to money; I am a poor

miserable sergeant; you have a house of your own; I can't even
afford a bicycle. You fry eggs for breakfast . . . I eat 'gari'. Look . . .
look at your appearance . . . your dress, your make-up, your jewellery . . .
everything about you sparkling like gold . . . Money . . . Money!

LORA: But I love you.

MART: Do we have to start that all over again?

LORA: Honest, I love you. I never have had that sincere feeling about
a man before . . . I never felt my chest heaving for any man,
Sergeant.

MART: You don't love me, Flora.

LORA: I do.

MART: You don't love me. I know. Maybe you admire me. But you
don't love me . . . because you cannot love any man.

LORA: Why?

MART: Because to you . . . LOVE IS MONEY!

LORA: Before your time . . . before I met you . . . yes. But believe me a
woman grows up . . . changes.

MART: How? You have never worked for anything in your life . . .
never suffered. Everything is thrown to you as cheap and easy as your
false smile. How can you ever hope to change now?

LORA: Please, Sergeant, please.

MART: I am sorry but I have toiled in life . . . suffered for everything.
I have had my experience the hard way. I must share life with
people who know what life's suffering is like.

Knock.

LORA: Shhh . . . quiet!

MART: A visitor at midnight?

LORA: Shhh . . .

MART: Expecting anybody?

LORA: No . . .

Knock.

MART: Stay clear . . . it must be a thief.

Knock. SERGEANT *swings open door.* INSPECTOR GOFIE *is thrown on stage.
He has a broadsword.*

FLORA: Inspector!

INSPECTOR: I'm fine . . . I'm fine . . . Sergeant?

MART: Yes, sir.

INSPECTOR: What are you doing here?

FLORA: I invited him.

INSPECTOR: You are on duty, right?

MART: Yes, sir.

INSPECTOR: Negligence of duty! It's a serious charge.

FLORA: Sit down, Inspector.

INSPECTOR: Give me whisky. Yes, negligence of duty is a very serious charge. What? What do I see here? [*Picks up empty glass and sniffs*] Sergeant!

SMART: Yes, sir?

INSPECTOR: Drinking on duty? Serious charge, very, very serious charge! Where is my whisky? [FLORA *serves whisky*] [*Drinks*] Yes. Drinking on duty is a very, very serious charge. [*Sits down heavily*] Ah! Now, what are you doing here?

FLORA: I invited him.

INSPECTOR: You did, eh? Good . . . good . . . [*Drinks*] Come close here, Sergeant!

SMART: Yes, sir.

INSPECTOR: Look . . . look down there.

SMART: Where, sir?

INSPECTOR: Your flap, fool! Close it!

SMART: God! This zip again.

INSPECTOR: Improper dressing . . . Third serious charge. Report to me tomorrow. Now, attention! March out! Right, left . . . Left, right! STOP!

SMART: Yes, sir.

INSPECTOR: Sergeant!

SMART: Yes, sir?

INSPECTOR: Your cap. Where is your cap?

SMART: My cap?

INSPECTOR: Yes, your police cap. A policeman on duty must always sport his cap. Here is mine; where is yours?

FLORA *rushes into bedroom; re-enters with* SMART's *police cap. She throws cap to* SMART. INSPECTOR *catches it in mid-air.*

INSPECTOR: Deceiving your superior officer . . . fourth serious charge. I will deal seriously with you tomorrow. Now . . . move! Left . . . right . . . Left . . . right. [*Exit* SERGEANT SMART] That gets rid of him!

FLORA: What do you want here?

INSPECTOR: You.

FLORA: At this time of the night?

INSPECTOR: Any time! Any time! Give me a pretty woman . . . a pretty woman with a flashy smile . . . any time! Now give me more whisky and I will file my report. But, first; here! A broadsword, an antiquity. Art . . . a special gift from me. There are no more wars left these day. Decorate your room with it. Now . . . more whisky.

FLORA: Here . . . drink and disappear.

INSPECTOR: Thanks, my good woman. Yes . . . yes; your television set, You'll get it tomorrow.

FLORA: [*Embraces him hard*] Oh, you're such a darling!

INSPECTOR: [*Laughs*] Ho ho, ho ho.

FLORA: Shhhh . . . listen!

INSPECTOR: What?

FLORA: Somebody at the door.

INSPECTOR: Wait! [*Tiptoes to door; swings it open.* SERGEANT SMART *is thrown on stage*]

FLORA: Sergeant!

INSPECTOR: Criminal . . . criminal!

SMART: I'm going now . . . I'm going . . . [*Exits*]

INSPECTOR: These small . . . small boys; they want what their fathers want, eh?

FLORA: What's the time, Inspector?

INSPECTOR: Is he gone now?

FLORA: He is gone.

INSPECTOR: Let me make sure. [*Moves to door*]

FLORA: Excuse me a minute.

INSPECTOR: Where are you going?

FLORA: I have to open the back window to my bedroom.

INSPECTOR: What for?

FLORA: Fresh air.

INSPECTOR: Wait a second. You are not going to allow that man into your bedroom through the back window, are you?

FLORA: [*Taps inspector on sensitive part*] Dirty old man.

INSPECTOR: [*Tickled*] Ho ho, ho ho . . . [*Drinks*] Ahh! You coming now?

FLORA: [*Offstage*] Just a minute.

INSPECTOR: [*Moves to centre table. Admires bouquet of fresh flowers*] Man! I like fresh things. Reminds me of my youth. Confirmation day . . . dresses all in white and those gay flower beds . . . and my box camera . . . snap . . . snap . . . Oh, the world grows up . . . too fast. [*Sings*] When I was just a little boy,

> I asked my father
> And he said:
> What will be; will be
> Qué será, será,
> What will be; will be . . .

Can't even remember those words any more . . . Where are you, ducky?

FLORA *enters. She has changed into something almost transparent.*

FLORA: Here.

INSPECTOR: Huuuuu . . .

FLORA: What is it?

INSPECTOR: I see you.

FLORA: Good . . . You've seen me. Good night!

INSPECTOR: Not so soon.

FLORA: It's late.

INSPECTOR: To sit close to me? It's never too late to . . . Sit down. Sit here.

FLORA: Good night!

INSPECTOR: Look . . . look what I have for you. [*Produces gold wrist watch*]

FLORA: Ohhh . . . beautiful! [*She sits*]

INSPECTOR: [*Pressing close*] It's for you. Gold. Solid gold.

FLORA: Mr Cofie!

INSPECTOR: Be a good girl . . . be a good girl . . . [*Bedroom door opens.* SERGEANT SMART *peeps*]

FLORA: Somebody will hear you.

INSPECTOR: Impossible!

FLORA: Let me go!

INSPECTOR: Every time I walk in here; every day I see you walk by . . . I want you!

FLORA: You're drunk, Inspector.

INSPECTOR: Don't go away! Don't leave me, ducky. I pay well! Anything . . . anything you want. Ask! It's yours!

FLORA: Please . . . I . . .

INSPECTOR: Why? Don't you like me? Here . . . [*Produces necklace*] Look . . . Look at it . . . it's yours. [FLORA *closes up.* INSPECTOR *embraces her*]

FLORA: No!

INSPECTOR: Every time I see you . . . You charge me up stiff . . . you make me feel young . . . you drive me . . .

Knock. Silence. Heavy knock.

FLORA: Who is it?

VOICE: Me. Charles.

INSPECTOR: Who is THAT?

FLORA: Charles? What do you want here at this time of night?

CHARLES: Just open the door.

FLORA: A moment. [*To* INSPECTOR] Hide in the kitchen.

INSPECTOR: What?

FLORA: Please.

INSPECTOR: No!

FLORA: That's my boy friend.

INSPECTOR: No.

FLORA: Try to understand.

INSPECTOR: In a kitchen? Never!

FLORA: Please.

INSPECTOR: No . . . No . . .

FLORA: If you refuse . . . take it that it's all over between us . . . Now, please.

Pause.

INSPECTOR: Alright. But I prefer the bedroom.

FLORA: [*Blocks bedroom entrance*] No; you can't go in there.

INSPECTOR: Why not? [*Knock*]

FLORA: Coming . . . [*To* INSPECTOR] Please.

INSPECTOR: Kitchen? No! Bedroom? YES!

FLORA: You don't understand. Charles left here a few hours ago. He left his tie in the bedroom.

CHARLES: Flora!

FLORA: Just a second.

INSPECTOR: Kitchen? No! I prefer to go away.

FLORA: [*Blocks exit*] Charles is right out there.

CHARLES: Who is in there with you?

FLORA: Nobody.

CHARLES: Open the door then.

FLORA: Coming . . . [*To* INSPECTOR] Please.

INSPECTOR: Alright.

FLORA: Thank you.

INSPECTOR: A kiss first.

FLORA: Here . . . [*Kisses him*] Now, in there . . . Go inside. [INSPECTOR *enters kitchen*]

FLORA: What a life.

CHARLES: Flooorrrrraaaaaaaa!!!!!!!!!

FLORA: Charles! [*Opens door. Enter* CHARLES)

CHARLES: Who is here with you?

FLORA: Nobody.

CHARLES: I heard a man's voice.

FLORA: A voice? Here? Oh . . . a voice . . . maybe from the radio. [*Turns radio off*]

CHARLES: What kept you so long opening the door?

FLORA: I was changing.

CHARLES: [*Admires transparent dress*] You really changed into something that I'd rather see you wear every day.

FLORA: What do you want here at this time of night?

CHARLES: I've come back.

FLORA: Back? What for?

CHARLES: [*Slumps down in comfort*] Forever.

FLORA: What do you mean 'Forever'?

CHARLES: I have been driven out there; I'm here to stay, forever.

FLORA: Your wife drove you out of your own house?

CHARLES: Yes, the sorceress. [*Laughs*] She thinks she's locked me out of my house, but you see, I have man's wit. I don't put all my eggs

into one basket. So let her take that house and all her foolishness.
I have you; I have here; I have a second home. Get me some
beer.

FLORA: Charles, I'm sorry. You can't stay here.

CHARLES: Can't?

FLORA: You can't.

CHARLES: You mean, the fact of my having a wedded wife? It's all over
now. Should be over this very week. I'm getting a divorce . . . And
why not? After all, she kicked me out of the house . . . I have never
loved her all along anyway.

FLORA: Go back to her. Now!

CHARLES: You get me some beer.

FLORA: You better leave now, Charles.

CHARLES: I bought this house, you know.

FLORA: Shall I call the police?

CHARLES: Strange. When I left here only a few hours ago you were all
warm, friendly and loving. What's happened? [CHARLES sees
half-filled drinking glass and bottle of whisky] Oh . . . I see . . . Who's in
here with you?

FLORA: Nobody.

CHARLES: That's a lie . . . Somebody's been drinking whisky here.

FLORA: I was drinking . . .

CHARLES: You're lying again. There is a man hiding in this house.

FLORA: What if there is? Am I your wife?

CHARLES: Wife or no wife, I bought this house.

FLORA: You bought that one too but you have been driven out of it.
Please go away.

CHARLES: What is this? What is happening tonight? How can a man
who's bought two houses be kicked out . . . and up and down
like . . .

FLORA: Shall I call the police?

CHARLES: [Grabs hold of broadsword] Over your very neck! Where is that
man hiding?

FLORA: Please put it away . . . put the sword away!

CHARLES: [Slaps her] Filthy whore! Where is he hiding?

FLORA: Don't hurt me . . . please!

CHARLES: Shut up! Where is he, I say!

FLORA: Please, Charles, go away!

CHARLES: Shut up! You are like all women after all!

FLORA: What of you, aren't you like all men?

CHARLES: [Slaps her] Shut up! A man is a man; he can have as many
women as he wants. Where is that man? Where is that thief
hiding?

FLORA: Help! Help, Sergeant!

CHARLES: [Attacks her] Who?

FLORA: Help, Inspector.

CHARLES: Inspector? [CHARLES *pulls out sword and slashes at her with it*]
Oh, you thieving harlot!

FLORA: Help! Help! He will kill me!

Enter SERGEANT SMART *from bedroom.*
Enter INSPECTOR COFIE *from kitchen.*

INSPECTOR: Sergeant?

SMART: Sir . . .

INSPECTOR: Still here?

FLORA: Oh . . . blood . . . blood . . .

INSPECTOR *drills* SERGEANT.
FLORA *moans and bleeds.*
CHARLES *bolts away.*

SMART: Sir, she's bleeding.

INSPECTOR: I've seen it. Why are you still here?

SMART: He's running away, sir . . .

INSPECTOR: I know that! Answer my question. How did you get into the
bedroom?

FLORA: Aooo . . .

SMART: Sir . . .

INSPECTOR: I know my work, Sergeant! And don't try to correct your
superior officer. You jumped through that window, right? Good, I'll
deal with you later. [*To* FLORA] Who was that man? What is his
name?

FLORA: Charles . . . Charles Brown, the city electrical engineer.

INSPECTOR: He is in serious trouble; I'll deal with him severely!
Sergeant!

SMART: Sir . . .

INSPECTOR: You still standing here? What are you waiting for? Get
that Charles! Arrest him! [*Sound of car taking off*]

SMART: He's got away, sir!

INSPECTOR: Use your head! Run after him; use your whistle; arrest
him! God! What is the service coming to?

SMART: He got away in a car, sir.

INSPECTOR: Get a car too; chase him!

SMART: You have the car key, sir.

INSPECTOR: Blockhead! I must chase him myself or nothing will ever get
done well.

SMART: What of her?

INSPECTOR: Of her?

SMART: Shall I stay here with her until . . .

INSPECTOR: Stay with her and play with her, eh? No, sir. We all go on the chase. Shakespeare says, 'A man cannot division himself into twice.' We cannot arrest for her and stay with her all at the same time. NOW MOVE!

Blackout. FLORA *still in pain.*

END OF FIFTH MOVEMENT

Final Movement

Sound of a car on the run. The car screeches to a halt. A car door bangs. Footsteps. Loud knock on stage door right.

VOICE: [*Offstage*] ELSIE! ELSIE! OPEN THE DOOR! [*Banging*] OPEN THE DOOR!

ELSIE: Who's that?

VOICE: Hurry up! Open the door!

ELSIE: Who're you?

CHARLES: It's me! Charles!

ELSIE: What do you want!

CHARLES: The police . . . the police . . . they're chasing me!

ELSIE: The what?

CHARLES: The police . . . they want me!

ELSIE: Wait a moment . . . I'm coming . . .

CHARLES: [*Banging with both hand and foot*] Hurry! Hurry!

ELSIE: I'm coming . . .

CHARLES: [*Banging*] Please!

ELSIE unlocks and opens door.

ELSIE: Well! What do you want?

CHARLES brushes past ELSIE. He is deeply frightened. His shirt is ripped in two at the back. His tie is unknotted and flying about. He carries a pistol and an African broadsword.

CHARLES: Please hide me!

ELSIE: Hide you . . . Charles! [*Sees the pistol*] What are you doing with . . . with . . .?

CHARLES: Help me! Hide me! The police . . . the police! [*Siren*]

ELSIE: What did you do to the police?

CHARLES: They want me! They're after me!

ELSIE: But what did you do? [*Siren*]

CHARLES: Where shall I hide?

ELSIE: You can't hide here . . . The police . . . I don't want anything to do with the police!

CHARLES: [*Checks pistol*] Well . . . they asked for it! I'll shoot and knife any . . . I'm not leaving . . . I am a man! I can fight!

ELSIE: You aren't going to fight the police in here.

CHARLES: They called the tune . . .

ELSIE: But the child . . . you don't want to shoot that gun here. Here . . . come here. Hide in here. In the wardrobe! [ELSIE *rushes* CHARLES *to wardrobe*]

CHARLES: The wardrobe is locked! [*Siren.* CHARLES *bangs at the wardrobe with his gun*]

ELSIE: The key is in the bedroom. I'll get it. [*Siren*]

CHARLES: They're here! They're here! [*Banging of door*] I'll hide in the bedroom.

ELSIE: The child is sleeping in there. [*Footsteps*]

CHARLES: I'll hide under the bed!

ELSIE: Hurry then! Hurry! They are here!

CHARLES: Thank you . . . thank you.

ELSIE: [*Pushes him into bedroom*] Hurry! [ELSIE *locks door and hides key in her brassiere. A loud knock from door right*]

VOICE I: [*Banging*] Open the door!

VOICE II: Mrs Brown, please open the door. It's the police.

ELSIE: [*Composes herself*] Who?

VOICE II: The police!

ELSIE: Anything I can do for you?

VOICE I: [*Louder banging*] Come on! Open the door there or I'll knock the damn thing off its hinges! [*Bangs*]

ELSIE: Alright! Alright! In a minute. I'm coming.

ELSIE *opens the door. A* POLICE INSPECTOR *and a* SERGEANT *enter.*
SERGEANT SMART *brushes past* ELSIE, *searching all over the room as if on a military expedition. He knocks the plastic flowers over.*

SMART: Where is he! Where is that bastard?

ELSIE: My flowers! My flowers!

SMART: [*Grabs hold of the flowers and whips* ELSIE *with them*] Where is he? Where is he?

ELSIE: God! Sergeant . . . Please . . .

INSPECTOR: Sergeant . . . Stop that!

SMART: Where is he?

INSPECTOR: Don't . . .

ELSIE: Who?

SMART: You know who I'm talking about! Where is that criminal!

ELSIE: Sergeant, you can't come crashing into a house, knock everything about . . . and . . . and . . . This is a respectable house. And I am Mrs . . .

SMART: Respectable house, my foot! [*Throws away plastic flowers*] Where is he hiding?

ELSIE: [*Runs for shelter*] Inspector, keep that man off me . . . I protest. I am Mrs Brown.

INSPECTOR: [*Strides forward with all dignity. Caning his left leg with his office staff with every step*] Sergeant, I take over.

MART: [*Protests*] Sir . . .

NSPECTOR: Disobeying orders?

MART: No, sir!

NSPECTOR: [*Collapses into chair*] Then shut up! [*Politely*] Sit down, Mrs Brown, please.

LSIE: Thank you.

NSPECTOR: [*Knocks at refrigerator*] Any . . . any beer in there?

MART: [*Protesting*] Sir . . .

NSPECTOR: Sergeant, am I in charge here?

MART: Yes, sir, but that's a dangerous man . . .

NSPECTOR: That's the more reason why, as Shakespeare says, 'We must careful be.'

LSIE *produces two bottles of beer.* INSPECTOR *selects a drinking glass for imself.*

NSPECTOR: I'll serve myself. I'll serve myself . . . Self service, first step to self discipline. [*Sits*] Oh . . . so tired . . . so tired and thirsty!

LSIE *gives a bottle of beer and drinking glass to* SERGEANT.

LSIE: Sergeant . . . some beer?

MART: I don't drink!

LSIE: Why do you try so hard to be unpleasant, Sergeant?

MART: Your husband. Where is he hiding?

LSIE: He is not in the house.

MART: Open all your doors! Open that wardrobe!

LSIE: This is a private house, Sergeant! You can't come in here and turn everything upside down like some savage. I won't have it!

NSPECTOR: Sergeant!

MART: [*Straightens up*] Yes, sir.

NSPECTOR: [*Drinks*] Gently . . . gently . . . police for peace! Peace Officers.

MART: Sir.

NSPECTOR: Am I in charge?

MART: Yes, sir.

NSPECTOR: Then, shut up! [*Drinks*] Mrs Brown, where is your husband?

LSIE: He's not in the house . . . He's not been to this house for three months!

MART: His car is parked outside.

LSIE: [*Sharply*] That's my car!

MART: Deceiving a public officer! Deceiving . . .

NSPECTOR: [*Drinks*] Sergeant! [*Pause. Drains last drop of beer. Stands up*] Now, Mrs Brown, bring your husband here.

LSIE: Sir, I'm telling the gospel truth! My husband has not been to this house.

INSPECTOR: Please, don't force me to have you roughed up. You are respectable . . . [*Cooking utensils fall in the kitchen*]

SMART: [*Rushes to kitchen door*] Who is in there, Inspector? There's a man in the refrigerator! [*Kicking door with foot*] Charles, I know you're in there!

ELSIE: Sergeant, my child is sleeping . . .

SMART: He is in there! [*Banging*] Charles, I know you're in there. Come out now! Come out or I'll come in and get you!

ELSIE: [*Opens kitchen door*] Look . . . look . . . there's nobody in there. [SMART *rushes into kitchen. Noise of pots and pans falling and knocking each other*] Oh God! Listen! The whole kitchen is . . . The man is mad! Mad!

INSPECTOR: One of his men was seriously wounded an hour ago. Policemen under pressure and danger can go mad.

Re-enter SMART. *He has some white powdery stuff in his hair and uniform.*

SMART: [*Furious*] Open that wardrobe!

ELSIE: I don't have the key!

SMART: Damn it! You have it! [*Pounces on* ELSIE] Give it to me!

ELSIE: You're squeezing . . . You'll kill me!

SMART: The key! The key!

ELSIE: Ahhh . . .

INSPECTOR: Softly . . . softly . . . Sergeant! Softly, softly catch the monkey!

SMART: [*Beside himself*] Charles, I know you're in there! Come out or I'll come in shooting . . .

ELSIE: Inspector, restrain that man! Keep him off my private property!

INSPECTOR: [*Restraining the* SERGEANT] Come, Sergeant Smart, cool off! Scotland Yard men never slapped a man but they are the most efficient policemen in the world. Come now, this way.

SMART: Sir . . .

INSPECTOR: Attention! [SMART *stiffens up*] Now, you speak when I ask you! We are dealing with educated people. This woman studied in London, you know! Please sit down, Mrs Brown.

ELSIE: [*Sophisticated*] Thank you, Inspector.

INSPECTOR: [*Sits*] Mrs Brown, I'd like to deal gently with you. But . . . your husband . . . almost killed a good woman . . . slashed her almost open with a broadsword.

ELSIE: Charles? No, Charles wouldn't do that.

SMART: You bring him out here.

INSPECTOR: Sergeant!

SMART: Yes, sir.

INSPECTOR: [*Picks up the second bottle of beer*] I'm sorry Mrs Brown. But eh . . . eh . . . sit down, sit down.

ELSIE: Thank you.

INSPECTOR: [*Opens beer*] You are the most respectable woman around this neighbourhood. I don't want to be too hard on you. But I have to explain to you that we are operating within the law. Your husband has broken the law; I must take him. Please, if he is in the wardrobe . . . bring him out!

ELSIE: Inspector, I give you my word, as I am a respectable woman, I haven't seen my husband for over three months.

MART: Sir, these are criminals! Why persuade them?

INSPECTOR: You see, Sergeant Smart wants his work fast and smart. Bring your husband here.

ELSIE: I swear to you . . . my husband is not here.

MART: Give me all the keys you have in the house.

ELSIE: [*Sharply*] I don't have any key!

MART: [*Flexing his muscles*] Sir, why do we entertain these criminals . . . give the order and I'll bring her back to her senses. Who does she think she is?

INSPECTOR: Mrs Brown, I told you the Sergeant is not a very polite man . . .

MART: I don't understand, sir; because they studied in England and London, because they can speak in a foreign tongue, and imitate foreign ways of life, they think they are special human beings. Sir, just say it . . . give me the order and I'll destroy all those sheepheads . . . these . . . [*Jumps on* ELSIE] Give me those keys!

ELSIE: Sergeant . . . Please . . . Please. Give me a little time.

MART: Damn you!

INSPECTOR: Shhh . . . Sergeant, quiet! There's somebody in that room?

MART: Which room?

INSPECTOR: [*Pointing to door centre*] That!

MART: [*To* ELSIE] Who's in there?

ELSIE: My child . . .

MART. Open the door.

ELSIE: It's my bedroom.

MART: Open the door.

INSPECTOR: [*Tries lock*] The door is locked. Why? Who is in there?

ELSIE: My child.

MART: Sir, she's telling a lie again! [*Shouts*] Charles! Charles! I know you're in there!

ELSIE: Terrorizing women and children . . . women and children . . . That's all the forces are good for! Go, take somebody your size . . .

MART: Come out of there or I'll smash my way in! Charles, I know you're in there! Don't attempt anything foolish . . . come out quietly and give yourself up.

INSPECTOR: Sergeant!

MART: Sir?

INSPECTOR: When persuasion fails, use force!

SMART: Yes, sir! Charles, come out now or I'm coming in . . . You have ten seconds . . . one . . . two . . . three . . .

CHARLES: Okay . . . Okay . . . I'm coming out . . . I'm coming . . .

SMART: No dirty tricks. Mrs Brown, stay clear of the door. Your husband is still armed.

ELSIE: Leave him alone! Leave Charles alone! Go and fight somebody of your own size. . .

SMART: Come out now. I'm counting five. One . . . two . . . three . . .

CHARLES: Okay . . . Okay . . . I'm coming out . . . I'm giving up . . .

Door swings open. CHARLES *wielding a broadsword slashes his way through, knocks* SERGEANT SMART *down.*

SMART: Ahhh . . .

ELSIE: No, Charles . . . Please don't . . . [*Slashes at her*]

Sword flashes.
INSPECTOR *takes cover.*
CHARLES *flees.*

SMART: I'm wounded.

ELSIE: Ahh . . .

INSPECTOR: Sergeant . . . What . . .?

SMART: Get him . . . don't let him get away.

INSPECTOR *blows whistle. Whistle sounds almost like kettle whistle, then fades away.* ELSIE *and* SMART *waiting and moaning in pain.*

ELSIE: Ahh . . . Blood . . . blood . . .

SMART: Shut up! That's what you assimilated people brought to us poor people . . . blood . . . blood . . . AND TEARS!

The hunt still goes on.

Blackout.

CURTAIN

AMMA PRANAA

A Folkstory Play

*If the porcupine says it will fight an
elephant, leave it alone to fight the
elephant: its quills will get finished.*

Note for directors

Music, drumming and dances and mimetic actions in the play are strictly
part of the development of the story. Translation of song from Akan into
English has been included to explain how songs fit into the narrative
structure. In production a director may have to compose songs and
choreograph dances to suit the ideas expressed.

Characters

AMMA PRANAA, *A very pretty girl*
AGYA AMOA, *Her father*
AWO ABENAA, *Her mother*
OBOFO, *The hunter*
KWAME, *A stranger*
MASTER DRUMMER
STORYTELLER
Chorus, Drummers and Audience

Bare stage. The lights begin to come on. Enter the MASTER DRUMMER, *his drum sticks under his armpit and tying his cloth properly around his waist. He studies the stage for a moment.*

MASTER DRUMMER: Hey, hurry up there with the drums! You can't waste too much of our good audience's time.

Enter four men carrying 'Atumpan' drums.

MASTER DRUMMER: Good, hurry. You two, fix the drums here, [*Stage right*] you and you, run up and bring . . . Let me see . . . one, two, three, four . . . four stools. Hurry up, we don't always have to be late in everything.

Lights dim. Exit all except MASTER DRUMMER. *Four or six members of the 'audience' enter and sit in the auditorium. Spotlight is thrown on the drums.*

MASTER DRUMMER:
    Kron! Kron! Kron!
    Listen, the Master Drummer speaks,
    The Tall Drummer whose name is 'Tweneboa Kodua';
    The estimable Master Drummer says;
    I have come from 'Kotoko'
    Where ever I have been;
    I was held in esteem.

    Kron! Kron! Kron!

    Faithful drum stick, carved of the great 'ofemma' tree;
    The unbreakable drum stick whose name is 'Sakyi';
    My condolence;
    Have my condolence for your trouble.

    Kron! Kron! Kron!

    Mother earth whose name is Yaa;
    Great mother earth who is made of dust;
    Great Mother earth who feeds on dead bodies.
    I sit on you at day time;
    I sleep on you at night;
    Mother earth, my condolence;
    Have my condolence for your troubles.

    Kron! Kron! Kron!

When did our creator create all things?
Our creator created all things long ago.
What did he create?
He created the 'Obua tree'[1]
And he created the Drummer.
The Drummer is aged and wise.
Aged and wise as creation.
He must be treated with reverence.

Kron! Kron! Kron!

Kron! Kron! Kron!
The estimable Master Drummer speaks;
The wise Master Drummer says:
Welcome; Welcome;
I welcome you all fellow noble men;
The great Master Drummer says;
Welcome . . .
AND ENJOY YOURSELVES WELL
Enjoy yourselves, 'Ahenewa'
Enjoy yourselves, 'Akudonto'
Enjoy yourselves well, 'Opeafo'
Kron! Kron! Kron!

Four stool are placed on stage right. Enter Players with drumming and dancing. Players dance all over and position themselves stage left.

[*Entrance song*]

CANTOR:	Ye de aba oo;	We have brought it
	Ye de aba . . .	We have brought it
	Anansesem yi	The Ananse[2] story,
	Ye de aba . . .	We have brought it.
CHORUS:	Ye de aba oo	We have brought it
	Anansesem yi	The Ananse story
	Ye de aba . . .	We have brought it.
CANTOR:	Anansesem a mmofra ne mpanyin nyinaa pe	The Ananse story, that is enjoyed by both the young and the old
	Ye de aba . . .	We have brought it.

---

[1] Obua tree: Tree used for carving drums.
[2] Ananse: Legendary hero in Akan trickster stories.

CHORUS:	Ye de aba oo	We have brought it
	Anansesem yi	The Ananse story
	Ye de aba	We have brought it.
CANTOR:	Anansesem a mpayin	The Ananse story that our elders
	de buu yen be	used to speak to us in proverbs
	Ye de aba	We have brought it.
CHORUS:	Ye de aba oo	We have brought it
	Anansesem yi	The Ananse story
	Ye de aba	We have brought it.
CANTOR:	Anansesem ntie-mmere	The story which one
	Ye de aba	Never tires listening to
		We have brought it.
CHORUS:	Ye de aba oo	We have brought it
	Anansesem yi	The Ananse story
	Ye de aba	We have brought it.

Enter the STORYTELLER. *He carries a linquist staff. Dances all over the stage.*

End of song. All are seated.

STORYTELLER: Well met, friends.

CHORUS: Thank you. Accept our greetings too.

STORYTELLER: I sincerely thank you.

1ST CHORUS What story are you telling us today?

STORYTELLER: What story do you want me to tell you?

1ST AUDIENCE: Tell us the story about Ananse and the ten thousand giants.

2ND AUDIENCE: No, tell us . . . eh . . . yes; tell us the story about Kwaku Ananse and Nana Nyankpong, the Creator.

2ND CHORUS: Ohh . . . you all leave him alone; let him tell us any story.

STORYTELLER: You want me to tell any story?

3RD CHORUS: No, why should you tell us just any story. We are not here to just laugh and forget . . . We are here to laugh and learn. So you'll tell us the story about that proud but pretty girl . . .

1ST CHORUS: Amma Pranaa?

3RD CHORUS: Yes, Amma Pranaa; that pretty but insolent girl who rejected the man her parents wanted her to marry and nearly met her death. The ever rebellious youth of today need it. They all need some talking to . . . in proverbs.

STORYTELLER: Do you all say that I tell you about Amma Pranaa and her marriage?

CHORUS AND AUDIENCE: Yes! Yes! Tell us that story. Yeees . . . Yesssssss [*Clapping of hands, etc.*]

STORYTELLER: Very well; is our cantor ready?

CANTOR: Here; and ready.

STORYTELLER: I see you're all ready and full of some spirit. I must get

ready too . . . ahh; this cloth too . . . [*Ties cloth properly around the waist*]
Now, let me have a song. Something good, something sweet to warm
me up.

CANTOR: Are you drummers ready?

CHORUS: Ready!

CANTOR: Really ready?

CHORUS: Yes!

CANTOR: Ahhh . . . today is today. I'll make you all sing us all to . . .
sleep. Now, women, your hands . . . clap now . . . a little harder.
Ahhh . . . get into it . . . let yourself go . . . enjoy it . . . like it . . .
like it . . . like that . . . swing left . . . now right . . . Ahh . . .
[*Breaks into song;* STORYTELLER *and other members of* CHORUS *dance*]

CANTOR: Wongye me nndwom oo;	Enjoy this my song
Wongye me nndwom oo;	Enjoy my song
Nngye me nndwom oo;	Enjoy my song
Nngye me nndwom	Enjoy this my singing
Amoa ba ee	About Amoa's (child) daughter.
CHORUS: Wongye me nndwom oo;	Enjoy my song
Wongye oo	Enjoy it.
CANTOR: Amoa ba ee	About Amoa's daughter.
CHORUS: Wongye me nndwom oo	Enjoy my song
Wongye oo	Enjoy it.
CANTOR: Asem bi a yede ba	The story that I am going to
Amoa ba ee	Tell about Amoa's daughter.
CHORUS: Wongye me nndwom oo	Enjoy my song
Wongye oo	Enjoy it.
CANTOR: Agori bi a yeredi,	The new play that we are going to
Amoa ba ee	to perform about Amoa's daughter.
CHORUS: Wongye me nndwom oo	Enjoy my song
Wongye oo	Enjoy it.
CANTOR: Nndwom bi yereto;	The new song that we have come
Amoa ba ee	to sing about Amoa's daughter.
CHORUS: Wongye me nndwom oo;	Enjoy my song
Wongye oo	Enjoy it.
CANTOR: Asaw bi a yeresaw;	The new dance that we have come
Amoa ba ee	to dance about Amoa's daughter.
CHORUS: Wongye me nndwom oo	Enjoy my song
Wongye oo	Enjoy it.
CANTOR: Amoa ba ee	Amoa's daughter.
CHORUS: Wongye me nndowm oo	Enjoy my song
Wongye oo	Enjoy it.

STORYTELLER: [*Mopping his brow*] Hww . . . ah . . . Well done. Well
done, 'Opeafo'. [*Centre stage*] Ananse stories are not to be fully
believed. We only take what we learn from it and throw the rest
away! If your elders ask you to mend your ways . . .

CHORUS: It is for your own good tomorrow.

STORYTELLER: The wise are spoken to in proverbs. Aprapraa oo . . .

CHORUS: Yoo . . .

STORYTELLER: Aprapraa oo . . .

CHORUS: Yoo . . .

STORYTELLER: Was it not a very very . . . very . . . very pretty girl . . .

CHORUS: Yeeessss . . . ehee . . . eeh . . . eeeeeeeth.

STORYTELLER: She's so pretty that when she looks into a mirror . . . her eyes alone can slit the mirror right up into two clear halves!

CHORUS: Yeeeeessss . . . yeeeeeee . . . [*Whistles etc.*]

STORYTELLER: Yes . . . she was so pretty she, I will say, she could tame a whole lion with just her one flashy smile.

CHORUS: [*Protests*] Ohh . . . No! . . . How?

STORYTELLER: You don't believe me?

CHORUS: No . . .

STORYTELLER: If you challenge me again I will produce her here right now.

CHORUS: Yess . . . go on . . . go on, etc.

STORYTELLER: . . . No . . . I won't. She'll charm you all . . .

CHORUS: No . . . no . . . no . . . [*Whistles, etc.*]

STORYTELLER: But . . . [*Long pause*]

CHORUS: Yessss . . .

STORYTELLER: I can see some young men straining to hear some more.

CHORUS: Yesss . . .

STORYTELLER: So I won't say any more about this pretty girl . . .

CHORUS: [*Protesting*] Ohh . . .

STORYTELLER: But . . . [*Pause*] . . . as the elders say, 'Beauty is more than what one sees in a woman's shapely legs and fat . . .'

AUDIENCE: Woso . . . woso . . .

General laughter.

STORYTELLER: If you are a pretty woman, I want to feel it from the bottom of your . . .

AUDIENCE: Soup . . .

CHORUS: [*Mimes eating tasty soup*] Hmmmmmm . . . hmmmmmm . . .

MEMBER OF CHORUS: [*Jumps from auditorium onto stage*] Hold your story there! I have a song . . .

Dedendee Kwaw ee	Dedendee Kwaw ee
Dedendee Kwaw ee	Dedendee Kwaw ee
Agya Obofo wo	Mr Hunter, your soup
Nkwan ye me de	Tastes good but your
Nanso w'atade	'Hunting attire' is
Ye me tan	Simply repulsive.

CHORUS *about to respond to song.*

[1] Behind

STORYTELLER: [*Cuts chorus off*] Thank you . . . thank you; you've been such enormous help. You have helped me pick my appetite. Now this cloth too . . . [*Ties it up properly*] You know, after so many years, some of us are still learning how to drape our cloth properly . . . Now . . . about this pretty girl. [*Enter* AMMA PRANAA] Ah, here she is . . . I told you, if you kept challenging me I was going to produce her and send the young men dreaming about her . . . Now you just look at her . . . look at such curves . . . such shape . . . such . . . such . . . isn't she grown up and pretty enough to brighten some man's dull home?

CHORUS: She is.

STORYTELLER: She really is. But she refuses to get married. Her parents have done everything in the world to attract her to some beautiful home but . . . No . . . she won't have it . . . All the princes and the quacks from Takyiman to Timbukto have tried to wed her but no . . . So one day her father . . .

Enter AGYA AMOAH; STORYTELLER *sits among the chorus.*

AGYA AMOA: Amma, we are still waiting.

AMMA PRANAA: I won't have him. And that's final.

AGYA AMOA: And I say, you're marrying him. That's my decision. And its final.

AMMA PRANAA: The matter is closed . . .

AGYA AMOA: You want to kill me . . . and your mother . . . What is it you're doing? We are both old. You are our only child.

AMMA PRANAA: If you two are both old that's no reason why I should sign myself to that worthless hunter. I am young and pretty; I deserve a much more presentable man.

AGYA AMOA: A pretty woman owes her beauty to her good husband. I am an old man, it is true; I have not, in all my lifetime seen a fish turn into a lizard or a man turn into a woman, but I have seen pretty young women, with wicked husbands, ageing twice as fast as their mothers. You are my only daughter and all that I have in the world. Let me help you choose your future.

AMMA PRANAA: No!

AGYA AMOA: No is no answer . . .

AMMA PRANAA: Fine then; I'll be plain. I will marry whom I choose; when I choose . . . and where I chose.

Enter AWO *and* OBOFO.

AWO: Amma, your husband is leaving now.

AMMA PRANAA: Don't come here with that.

AWO: I am on my knees to you; please, listen to the cry of your poor old mother. Please, see him off.

AMMA PRANAA: He found his way here himself, he can find his way out!

AWO: You are not going to disgrace me, Amma. Look at me, your own mother; I'm down on my knees to you . . . down on my knees to you.

AGYA AMOA: Amma, look, your own mother is on her knees . . . or would you have me too . . . [*About to go down to his knees*]

OBOFO: [*Prevents* AGYA AMOA] No, Father.

AGYA AMOA: Let me go down to her, if that will soften her hardened heart.

OBOFO: No, Father, if you cannot pick a green palm nut, you wait until it is red and ready. Don't put pressure on Amma. I am waiting until she's ready.

AMMA PRANAA: And what does that mean?

OBOFO: I am a man; I must have patience.

AMMA PRANAA: Then keep your patience in your house and don't come here again.

OBOFO: Agya, I am leaving now, [*Shake hands*] and thank you for everything. Awo, thank you for your kindness. [*Exit* OBOFO]

AGYA AMOA: Amma.

AMMA PRANAA: Don't call me.

AWO: Awuraa Amma.

AMMA PRANAA: I don't want to hear anything from you.

AGYA AMOA: [*To* STORYTELLER] My good friend, you know my trouble, tell me, what must I do? My only daughter refuses my advice; she insults me; she insults her mother; drives out her future husband . . . what shall I do?

STORYTELLER: Well, I shouldn't interfere in your family affairs but since you asked for my advice, I will say that there are many willing young men in the audience. Since Amma insists on choosing her own husband, I suggest that she looks around now, and picks one of these handsome young men. [*To* CHORUS] What do you say, young men?

MALE CHORUS AND MALE AUDIENCE: Yes, we are ready.

A WOMAN CHORUS: But you are already married.

THE MEN: So what, has anybody asked you anything? You are too known!

STORYTELLER: Amma, the young men here welcome you. Make your choice.

There is drumming. The young men step out one after the other. Each dances to AMMA *and carries on a pantomimic dance, showing his love for her. They are all refused. End of drumming and dancing.*

MALE CHORUS: [*Disappointed and angry*]
            Who are you at all?
            You are too proud.
            You are just a woman.
            Do you think you deserve a man like me?
            We shall all like to see the beauty who marries you.

STORYTELLER: Good friends, do not be annoyed with Amma. She is still a child. You don't measure a woman's maturity by the size of her breasts. She still acts like a child. But allow her to preen.

A WOMAN CHORUS: Yes, but we women are like the morning flower, we must attract the bee while still fresh.

A MAN CHORUS: You don't mind her; the cunning bird is caught with a dry plantain fibre. Leave her to think still that . . .

AWO: Don't curse my daughter with your foul tongue, on an early morning like this. Amma, come to your mother.

AGYA AMOA: Abenaa, fetch me my gourd of palm wine. [*Exit* AWO] I must pour libation to our guardian spirit before I say anything more. Amma, fetch yourself a stool and sit down.

AWO: [*Enters*] Here is your palm wine.

AGYA AMOA: Thank you. Find yourself a seat.

The storyteller joins him. AGYA AMOA *mimes libation pouring in stylized movement.*

LEADER: Nana ee yegu nsa oo; nsa ni oo
Nana Nyame ye gu nsa oo; nsa oo
Nana ee yegu nsa oo; aeeeee

Grandfather here is drink
God our grandfather this is for you
Grandfather here is drink.

LEADER: Atenase ope; Nana Nyame yegu nsa oo

Almighty God our grandfather;
Here is drink.

CHORUS: Atenase ope . . .

Hear us.

LEADER: Aduana Mpayinfo, nsa ni oo

'Adua' Elders, here is drink.

CHORUS: Atenase ope . . .

Almighty grandfather; hear us.

LEADER: Asase Yaa nsa ni oo

Mother earth; here is drink.

CHORUS: Atenase ope . . .

Hear us; almighty grandfather.

LEADER: Ayokofo Nsamanfo ee nsa ni

'Ayokofo' spirits; here is yours.

CHORUS: Atenase ope . . .

Hear us; almighty grandfather.

LEADER: Asonafo Nsamanfo nsa ni oo

'Asonafo' spirits; this is for you.

CHORUS: Atenase ope . . .

Hear us; almighty grandfather.

LEADER: Nananom mpayinfo atena se oo ee

Elders, I welcome you all here.

CHORUS: Atenase ope . . .

Hear us; almighty grandfather.

LEADER: Aee ee Odense ee;
Yesre mo gyinabea oo

Greatest of all great gods
Please give us life fruitful.

CHORUS: Eee Odense ee

Greatest of great gods

LEADER: Nananom ye yesre mo Gyinabea	Grandfathers we ask life abundance.
CHORUS: Eee Odense ee	Hear us; greatest of great gods.
LEADER: Asase Yaa, Odense na yesre no gyinabea oo	Mother Earth, great goddess, we ask for fruitful life.
CHORUS: Eee Odense ee	Greatest of great gods Hear us.

AGYA AMOA: [*Drinks from calabash*] Hwween!!

STORYTELLER: 'Dahwe', a strong man does not panic in time of trouble.

AGYA AMOA: [*Resumes seat*] Now, Amma, are you there?

AMMA: I am here.

AGYA AMOA: Listen carefully to what I am going to say.

AWO: Bring your stool closer here.

AMMA: I can hear him!

AWO: Listen to the way she talks to her mother, ah . . .

AGYA AMOA: Amma.

AMMA: Father.

AGYA AMOA: Close your eyes.

AMMA: Why?

AWO: Just do as he says.

AMMA: Well, I have.

AGYA AMOA: Open your eyes.

AMMA: Why?

AWO: Just do what he says.

AMMA: I have.

AGYA AMOA: What did you see?

AMMA: Darkness.

AGYA AMOA: And when you saw the darkness, did you sleep?

AMMA: No, Father.

AGYA AMOA: Good. When one sees darkness, it does not mean one is asleep.

AMMA: I don't get your meaning, Father.

AGYA AMOA: If all is well in the home, one does not speak to a child in proverbs.

AMMA: I still don't understand anything.

AGYA AMOA: If the elder has nothing at all . . . he has an elbow. Bring your chair close here and listen to me with all your attention.

AMMA: I have . . .

AGYA AMOA: You are my only daughter and are therefore like one precious egg in one's hand. If I handle you well, you can hatch and multiply and pass on my name to following generations. If I allow you to slip and fall, everything is lost. I cannot even lick the stain from the dust. My house, my name . . . everything.

AWO: We are concerned about your future; we are also concerned about

the future of the family. Give this last honour to your father.
Marry Obofo.

AMMA PRANAA: I knew what you two were driving at when you began.
Don't waste so much breath. Leave me to my own choice. I am old
enough to find myself my own man.

AGYA AMOA: You women are yet to learn the cunning nature of men.

AWO: What is wrong with Obofo anyway?

AGYA AMOA: That he is not handsome? Men are not jewels; goodness is
not in what you see in a man's shining face. Good name, kindness,
love and honesty, these are the cherished. Think carefully about
Obofo.

AWO: Disease, thieves, murderers, liars, these are all in the blood; they
are inherited. Marry a murderer and all your children are going to
be murderers.

AGYA AMOA: Obofo comes from a decent home, free from all disease and
bad conduct. We cannot force you into this but you would make
us . . . me and your mother, happy if you would accept him as your
husband. [*Long pause*] Well . . . Amma, I'm listening to you.

AMMA: But . . . But . . . [*Stops short. Breaks out weeping*] But . . .

AWO: [*To* AGYA AMOA]: You see . . .

AGYA AMOA: Let her weep.

AWO: Stop child . . . stop . . . here [*Gives her cover cloth*] Wipe your tears
with this.

AMMA: [*Speaking through tears*] It isn't that I don't want to marry but . . .

AGYA AMOA: But what?

AMMA: I will get married eventually.

AGYA AMOA: I know . . . but when?

AWO: Wipe your tears and tell him.

AMMA: Soon.

AGYA AMOA: How soon?

AMMA: The day is not long off . . .

AGYA AMOA: Yes! If the old woman goes to the riverside to fetch
water . . . she will come back alright but . . . TIME . . .

AWO: You too don't pester my daughter; she's been trying to decide

AGYA AMOA: She's been trying to decide for the past five years . . .

AWO: It is only today we have really confronted her with the real issue.
Give her a little more time.

AGYA AMOA: A little more time . . . a little more time! I have been
giving her a little more time for the past five years! Why? Doesn't
she have an opening between her legs? You talk to her; I don't want
to see her face again.

AWO: Amma, you see . . .

AGYA AMOA: I have washed my hands of her! Clean!

AWO: Amma . . . say something!

AMMA: You will know when the day comes.

AWO: How are we to know?

AMMA PRANAA: You will know by this sign. If on that day, Father is smoking his pipe as he is doing now, I will pull the pipe from his mouth and break it in two. Or if he is drinking palm wine, I will take the calabash from him and hit him on the head with it.

CHORUS: Yoo . . . we have heard you and will watch out for the great sign.

WOMAN CHORUS: [*Shakes hands with* AMMA] Amma, let me wish you all the luck in your search. But as a woman, allow me to say this. We women are too dormant to match the wiles of men. I would your parents were allowed to make this one sacred choice for you; but since you, a woman, have hit your hand against your chest on this matter, watch out for the deceptive nature of man.

AMMA PRANAA: I am too wise to be fooled.

A MAN CHORUS: Let's hope so.

STORYTELLER: So Agya Amoa and his wife Awo Abenaa, retired to their house to wait patiently for the day when Amma Pranaa would come and announce her husband. [*Exeunt* AGYA AMOA; AWO ABENAA: AMMA PRANAA] But look friends, our elders were not lying when they said that the human tongue is like an amulet; whatever you wish with it will come true. Months have gone by, Agya Amoa and his wife have given up any hope about Amma's promise. But at times, it is when we have no food left in the house that we receive visitors. It is the end of another year. Today is a big festival day. All the young men and women in the villages around are dressed in their best clothes. Amma Pranaa is here too. Just look at her.

Drumming and dancing. Sikyi: Flirtatious dance. (Dance consists of little running steps and hops. The beginning position: the dancer stands with the left leg back, hands raised forward or to the side. Hand gestures must be flexible and, as the dancers move to the rhythm of the drums, there is natural shifting of weight from the right foot to the left with alternating forward body bending movement. Dance must be done in pairs.)
Enter AMMA PRANAA. *She dances alone. Enter a handsome stranger. He dances to* AMMA. *They go through the various stages of the flirtatious dance. By the end of the dance* AMMA *is wooed. She rushes off the stage with the young man. Enter* AGYA AMOA: Honest . . . I don't.

CHORUS: Ahh . . . here they come. Agya Amoa and Awo, we share your joy.

AGYA AMOA: Are you talking to us?

CHORUS I: My prayer is that he will become like the husband my parents chose for me.

AGYA AMOA: I don't understand you.

CHORUS II: Whatever pillow you slept on yesterday, sleep on it again today.

AGYA AMOA: I still don't get your meaning.

CHORUS III: As if he doesn't know what we are talking about.

AGYA AMOA: Honest . . . I don't.

CHORUS I: Buy us some palm wine; we are thirsty.

AGYA AMOA: Abenaa, bring them some palm wine. [*Exit* AWO. AGYA AMOA *calls* CHORUS II *aside*]

AGYA AMOA: I know you will tell me everything. What is it you have been trying to tell me?

CHORUS II: I would like to tell you but . . . your daughter, you know her temper.

AGYA AMOA: I won't tell her you told me anything.

CHORUS: Why don't you sit down and relax?

AGYA AMOA: How can I relax?

CHORUS: You will know everything soon.

AGYA AMOA: Yes but how soon?

CHORUS II: Don't worry, Agya Amoa, everything that goes up comes down.

CHORUS III: Agya Amoa, where is the palm wine?

AGYA AMOA: Don't bother me about palm wine! I am thinking!

CHORUS I: Then sit down; smoke for a while and relax. You can think better that way.

AGYA AMOA: You are right . . . right. I relax better on tobacco.
[AGYA AMOA *sits and begins to smoke*]

MASTER DRUMMER:
Kron! Kron! Kron!
We share your joy;
We share your sorrow;
Agya who is ever right.
A word from an elder
Is more powerful than an amulet.
The Master Drummer says;
I have come not to praise;
But if the elder has nothing at all;
He has his elbow.
Amma, watch your next step carefully;
If you skin the ant with patience,
You see its intestines.
Kron! Kron! Kron!

Enter AWO.

AGYA AMOA: What does that mean?

CHORUS III: Hey, Awo, I am here. Bring the palm wine over here.

AGYA AMOA: Bring it here first. [*Takes calabash*] Now . . . pour . . .

[*Drinks*] Hwwww . . . Awo Yaa; the black ant says, if God falls from heaven he will catch him. Let me chase that one with another.
[*Pours wine for himself. Enter* AMMA PRANAA. *She pulls the pipe from* AGYA'*s mouth and breaks it*]
Hey! You broke my pipe! What is wrong with you?

AMMA PRANAA: Shhhhhhh . . .

AWO: Could this mean . . .?

AGYA AMOA *drinks;* AMMA *takes the calabash from his mouth and hits him on the head with it.*

AGYA AMOA: Wui . . . wui . . . wui . . . what is wrong with . . .? [*Exit* AMMA PRANAA]

AWO: The signal, the signal I have been waiting for for years! At last!

AGYA AMOA: What signal?

AWO: Have you forgotten?

AGYA AMOA: All your talking don't make sense today!

AWO: Could you have forgotten so soon about the promise Amma made to you? Oh, could it be that my daughter has met some young handsome man she's taken a liking to?

AGYA AMOA: [*Interested*] Hm . . . what are you saying?

AWO: At last, I am going to have a grandchild.

AGYA AMOA: Eh? Did that spoiled child get married and not tell her father?

AWO: Ah, 'Abosom', let him be a rich young handsome man. I must kill a fowl and sprinkle mashed yam on Nana Tano today.

STORYTELLER: Why don't you go inside and prepare to meet the man?

AGYA AMOA: But I don't know the man.

STORYTELLER: We all don't know him. But I am sure he is waiting in the house to meet you, like a dutiful son-in-law. Hurry now.

AGYA AMOA: Yes . . . hurry. Let's go to the house and meet . . . well, I don't know his name.

CHORUS *begins to hum 'Dedendee'.*

STORYTELLER: Never mind about his name; some men carry their story with them. That is what you must be watchful about.

AGYA AMOA: Let's go in, Abenaa, and . . .

AWO: Yes, Let's go . . . and I haven't even got a white clay in the house . . . [*Exit* AGYA AMOA *and* AWO]

STORYTELLER: So Amma Pranaa brought her young lover home to meet her parents. He is a very handsome young man. But not all beautifully ripe fruits taste sweet. And men are like fruits; sometimes the most beautifully ripe ones are badly rotten in the inside. The worst of our men today are the handsome ones. But if the elder has nothing at all, he has an elbow. Agya Amoa and Awo Abenaa sized this young man up and refused there and then to give their daughter to him. But when a woman is in love, she becomes as stubborn as a he-goat. Amma must have her way. A day was fixed when the young man was to perform all the customary rites and take his wife away. Every member of the family and all the neighbourhood had been invited. You watch . . .

AUDIENCE: 'Akora', hold on to your story. [*A man from the audience jumps on stage. Takes off his cloth, revealing his costume. Enter* KWAME, AMMA PRANAA, AGYA AMOA *and* AWO ABENAA.] I was there that day at the ceremony and saw how friends and relatives bearing gifts for Amma came there singing. [*Sings*]

Dedende, ye nnim no oo.	Dedende,[1] we don't really know him
Dedende, ye nnim no oo.	Dedende, we don't really know him
Dedende, ye nnim no oo.	Dedende, we don't really know him
Ye nnim no; Kwame	Don't know him; Kwame

CHORUS: Dedendee ye nnim no oo — Dedende, we don't really know him;

AUDIENCE: Obiba Iron boy; — That handsome young man

CHORUS: Dedendee ye nnim no oo — Dedende, we don't really know him

AUDIENCE; Ne kon te se Adenkum — He is slim and handsome like 'Adenkum'

CHORUS: Dedende, yenn im no oo — Dedende, we don't really know him

AUDIENCE: Na aniwa te se ahwehwe — His eyes are as clear as the mirror.

CHORUS: Dedende, ye nnim no oo — Dedende, we don't know him.

AUDIENCE: Nehwene te se kyerewdua — The nose as pointed as a pencil.

CHORUS: Dedende, ye nnim no oo — Dedende, we don't really know him

AUDIENCE: Ne se te se asikire — His teeth are as white as sugar.

CHORUS: Dedendee, ye nnim no oo — Dedende, we don't really know him.

As the song goes on some members of the CHORUS *exit and re-enter carrying presents for the bride. They put the presents down and dance slowly with their hands on their head, moving the head back and forward to a slow tempo. The whole movement should suggest grief. While this is going on in the background, (all in stylized movement) the young man,* KWAME, *gets up. Pours a drink, sips and gives it to* AMMA. *He produces a short piece of specially carved 'Ofo' wood; gives it to* AGYA AMOA; AGYA AMOA *accepts it, by touching the wood to his chest.* AGYA AMOA *passes the 'Ofo' to* AWO, *who accepts it and passes it on to*

---

[1] Dedende means 'but' in the above context.

other members of the family; finally to AMMA, *who keeps the carving.* AMMA
pours a drink, sips it and gives it to KWAME. *Next,* KWAME *produces a bag of
cowris, presents it to* AGYA AMOA, *who handles it to feel the weight and passes
it on to* AWO *until it finally reaches* AMMA. *Two other bags of cowries are produced
and passed round; one kept by the head of the family and the other by* AWO
ABENAA. *The music swells as more gifts pour in.* AWO *weeps as* AMMA *is led
offstage by* KWAME. *Drumming ceases*

CHORUS: We wish you a thousand luck in your new home. May he be
    fertile and strong to give you twins every year.
CHORUS I: Condolence, take my condolence, Amma, for your lost honour.
    Your long preserved virginity will soon be no more.
CHORUS II: I pray for you, Amma, that he may be strong, kind and
    industrious. Marriage that makes the woman a virtual slave is what
    I pray does not happen to a good woman like you.
CHORUS III: Stop inviting hard luck with your tongue. Any wish that
    comes from a mouth that knows the feel of pepper and salt comes
    true.
MASTER DRUMMER:
    Kron! Kron! Kron!
    The river crosses the path;
    The path crosses the river
    Which of you is the elder?
    We cut a path and found the river
    The river came long long ago.
    It came from the creator of all things.
    Kron! Kron! Kron!
CHORUS I: What is the meaning of your wise saying, Prince of
    Wisdom?
CHORUS II: I don't get the meaning.
CHORUS III: The Master Drummer has spoken, it is meant for those who
    have ears to hear.

INTERLUDE. Enter two men, one blind and the other deaf.

BLIND MAN: Kofi, Kofi run over here. Come over here. I have found
    something beautiful.
DEAF MAN: What did you say you have?
BLIND MAN: Are you deaf? I said, I have found something.
DEAF MAN: Who is deaf?
BLIND MAN: You come over and see what I have in my hand.
DEAF MAN: What is it?
BLIND MAN: You come over and see.
DEAF MAN: [*Goes near*] Alright, here I am. Let me see it.
BLIND MAN: No, guess what it is first.
DEAF MAN: Well . . . is it a pebble?

BLIND MAN: Eyes but no eyes. Try again.

DEAF MAN: Is it money?

BLIND MAN: Who throws money away like that these days? Try again.

DEAF MAN: What is it then?

BLIND MAN: [*Opens his hand*] Look at it.

DEAF MAN: Okay, I have seen it; Now you tell me. What is it?

BLIND MAN: Can't you see? Look at it, it is a bead, an angry bead.

DEAF MAN: But you are blind; how did you know it was an angry bead?

BLIND MAN: Who is blind?

DEAF MAN: I am.

BLIND MAN: How dare you call me blind!

DEAF MAN: But you can't see.

BLIND MAN: What of you who can't hear anything at all?

DEAF MAN: How dare you!

BLIND MAN: But it is true. You are deaf.

DEAF MAN: You are out of your mind. If I am deaf, how is it that I am hearing you?

BLIND MAN: And if I am a blind man, how did I find the angry bead?

DEAF MAN: Alright . . . alright, you can't see but you are not blind. Let's leave the matter there.

BLIND MAN: Then you too, you are deaf but you can hear. Let's leave everything here.

Enter STORYTELLER.

CHORUS: Hey . . . the storyteller is back. You two good-for-nothing people, vanish from here.

STORYTELLER: There is no such thing as a good-for-nothing human being. One is blind and the other is deaf but everyone is useful in his own way. Have you heard the story about the fool who saved his father from death after all his wise brothers had failed in their attempt to save him?

CHORUS: No.

STORYTELLER: Would you like to hear it?

CHORUS: Yes, yes, of course.

STORYTELLER: Alright. Join us here again tomorrow night. I will be here again with another very interesting story[1] . . . and bring your friends. Don't fail me, bring more of your friends tomorrow, because I am not going to fail you. I shall tell an even more beautiful story. [*To the* BLIND MAN *and the* DEAF MAN] You two can find some place to sit. You can sit among the audience if you wish. [*They sit*]. Now to go on with our story . . . where was I?

CHORUS I: Where Amma Pranaa married . . . no, it was after the marriage and . . .

---

[1] See *Piesie*, my second folkstory play.

STORYTELLER: Yes, I have got it. Thank you. So Amma and the stranger married. The marriage ceremony has come to an end, and the custom demands that Amma stays with her parents for three months. But she will not listen to it. Her husband was leaving the following day and Amma Pranaa was determined to go with her husband.

Exit a man from the CHORUS. *He re-enters with a cut-out tree and places it upstage centre.*

STORYTELLER: So Amma Pranaa left her home to find a new life with her husband. As soon as they left the house Amma's husband produced some powdery stuff, sprinkled a little on Amma and the job was done. Amma became insensible, like a she-goat, following her husband wherever he goes. They walked, and walked, and walked, and walked . . .

A MALE CHORUS: 'Akora', hold on to your story. When I sing, you will respond, 'Aboa ne dua, ye kura mu oooo.'

MALE CHORUS:	Aboa ne dua	The animal's tail
	Aboa ne dua	The animal's tail
	Ye kura mu oo	We are holding fast to the animal's tail
	Osebo ne dua mu	The lion's tail.
CHORUS:	Aboa ne dua	
	Aboa ne dua ye kura mu oooooooooo.	We are holding on to it fast
MALE CHORUS:	Gyata ne dua mu	The leopard's tail
CHORUS:	Aboa ne dua	
	Aboa ne dua ye kura mu oooooooooo.	We are holding on to it fast
MALE CHORUS:	Nini ne dua mu	The python's tail

Enter a man and a woman from CHORUS. *Man is dressed as lion with tail behind. Woman holding on to tail. They circle tree several times to suggest journey. Woman mimes tiredness and collapses; the man stands over her laughing.*

STORYTELLER: [*Continues*] . . . and walked for days until Amma was tired and hungry. And still they were walking. Neither says anything to the other and neither stops to eat or to drink even water. [*Exit members of* CHORUS. *Enter* KWAME *and* AMMA PRANAA. *They go round the tree*] Amma became afraid and suspicious. She wished she could go back home . . . but how? It is true when our elders said that if a child does what an elder does, he sees what an elder sees. This is no place for women, but before you create a dangerous situation for yourself, you must know how to get out of that situation.

Amma must summon courage and ask her husband to tell her something.

AMMA PRANAA: My husband . . . I am tired. Can't we have a little rest?

KWAME: Keep walking. We must be home before dawn.

AMMA PRANAA: But I am tired . . . I can't walk any further. [*Sits*]

KWAME: You can sleep then. I am not tired. I am going . . . [*They circle around the tree*]

STORYTELLER: Amma must follow her husband. They walked for hours until they came to a very thick forest . . . [*Re-enter member of* CHORUS. *Adds two more cut-out trees*]

. . . and here the footpath came to an end. Kwame, Amma's husband, pointed his hand to the forest and said to Amma:

KWAME: Here is where we are going. Just follow me . . . we shall be home soon.

AMMA: But there is no footpath to follow. And it is dark too.

KWAME: You just follow me and not another word!

AMMA: I am hungry and tired.

KWAME: If you are not coming, I am going. I must get home before dawn and feed my young ones. They have gone without a good meal for weeks.

AMMA: The young ones? Do you have children? You never told me you were married.

KWAME: You never asked me. Hurry! The children must be hungry, don't waste time.

AMMA: I can't understand you. It is three days since we started this journey . . . and all along you have only been laughing and whistling to yourself; you haven't eaten . . .

KWAME: A man picks up his appetite best when he is most hungry . . . Hurry . . . I am almost hungry now.

AMMA: I don't understand.

KWAME: You will understand everything soon.

AMMA: Understand what?

KWAME: Keep moving! We must be home before dawn.

AMMA: I am not moving an inch from here.

KWAME: I say, move on!

AMMA: To where? You told me you live in a big town. What big town can there be in the middle of a thick forest like this?

KWAME: Isn't a big forest much like a big town? The wild beasts like you people, the huge trees like your mansions? There is no difference between a wild beast and a human being, a jungle or a city. [*Pointing*] This is home too . . . get up, we must move on.

AMMA: To where?

KWAME: Home.

AMMA: Home in the heart of a jungle?

KWAME: Maybe. Get up now and follow me.

AMMA: You will have to kill me first. [KWAME *laughs loudly*] [AMMA *senses something unnatural*] What is that? [*The laughter sounds more like the roaring of a lion*]

KWAME: The hour is fast approaching when I must change to my real self. Get up! Follow! Hurry or you will see something that no pair of human eyes has ever seen before.

STORYTELLER: Friends, there are more strange things on this earth than meet the eye. The handsome young man who met, danced, wooed, and married beautiful Amma Pranaa was not a human being. HE IS A LION, a real lion that had temporarily borrowed a human form, for only three days. It is late in the night now, and the time when all animals come out of hiding; it is time too when Amma's husband, Kwame, must shake off his human form.

Drumming, jerky and loud with no basic movement. Mimes a lion circling and taunting its prey. Drumming ends.

KWAME: [*Now with a changed voice*] You have enough time to rest before I come back. I am going a few yards from here to call my little ones here. [*Laughs loudly*] They must be hungry. Your pride will soon come to a deserving end. [*Laughs loud*] And don't fool yourself by thinking you can run away. I am the King of the Forest. I smelled your pride miles from here; try to run away and you'll see that I can smell your stupidity anywhere around here. [*Laughs*] [*Exits*]

STORYTELLER: What can a woman do all alone by herself in such a thick forest and on a night like this?

CHORUS: Nothing but . . . weep.

STORYTELLER: Yes, nothing but weep. So Amma wept . . . and wept and at times sang.

AMMA PRANAA: Is this the end of beautiful Amma, that I should be led to die in a strange place where even my bones will not be found and given a decent burial? Oh . . . oh . . . Father said it but I did not listen; Mother said it but I did not listen. [*Sings*]

Agya kae oo; okae na mantie	Father said it; I did not take his advice.
Enna kae oo; okae na mantie	Mother said it; I did not take her advice.
Madi me koma akyi	I have allowed my temper to take the better side of me.
De me nsa apem me bo	Me, a woman has hit her hand on her chest hard;
ama aka me koma	And touched my heart itself
Me Amma Pranaa; Menko aware a;	Amma Pranaa; I married
M'ako ware kwae ase Hene	And married the King of the Forest

Meto mani hwe nifa aa;	I turn right; I see black
mehu no tumm;	
Meto mani hwe benkum a;	I turn left; I see red
me hunu koo;	
Odomankoma Owu; me ye	'Odomankoma' death; I am your slave.
wo akoa	
Fa me na me nkoda	Take your share; I want to rest.

STORYTELLER: It was pathetic. All hope was lost. But if Odomankoma has not decreed your death, you do not die. It so happened that Obofo, the hunter, was on this very night hunting in that same forest. He heard somebody singing and weeping in the forest. 'Who is that singing and weeping in a forest at this time of the night?' he asked himself. He was a bit afraid but he is the man who goes to where the gun booms. Obofo must go and find out. Just about this time, the lion had called all its cubs and they were swearing and laughing and happy on their way to feast on their prey. [*Enter* OBOFO, *right; and lion, left*] They both got to where Amma was weeping at the same time. I leave you to find out who is the real MAN.

The Hunters Dance: Hunter waves a whisk; dances round playing hide-and-seek game with the Lion. Takes his gun from his shoulder, aims at the Lion; a hide-and-seek game. Aims at the Lion; the Lion tries pouncing on the hunter; gun shot. The Lion fall and dies.

STORYTELLER: [*Shakes hands with Obofo*] You have done well. You have proved yourself well, Obofo.

OBOFO: [*Takes* AMMA's *hand*] You are saved, whoever you are. Tell me where you live and I will take you to your home.

AMMA PRANAA: Am I dreaming; am I in my right mind? What happened? A man; a human . . .

OBOFO: Yes, a human being. You are saved.

AMMA PRANAA: No, you have changed again. Kill me now. Kill me, I want to die.

OBOFO: You are frightened. Let me take you home.

AMMA PRANAA: But who are you? Where are you taking me to?

OBOFO: I am Obofo. Come now, I will take you home. The lion is dead and all the cubs have routed.

AMMA PRANAA: Obofo . . . Obofo.

OBOFO: Yes, Obofo, the hunter. And who are you?

AMMA PRANAA: I am the proud girl, Amma Pranaa.

OBOFO: Amma Pranaa! But what are you doing here at this time of the night?

AMMA PRANAA: Please take me home. There are many things the human mouth can't utter. Please take me to my father and my mother.

OBOFO: Yes, I will take you home.

AMMA PRANAA: Please.

STORYTELLER: And so Amma Pranaa was saved and restored to her parents. Agya Amoa and Awo Abenaa welcomed their daughter home, but not for long. As for Obofo . . . well you know, you cannot frighten a witch with red colour. A man is like the goat who says 'Where there is blood there is plenty of food.' Obofo kept visiting Amma regularly . . . and not long afterwards they were man and wife. They lived very happily. That is why our elders say *if the porcupine says it will fight an elephant, leave it alone to fight the elephant; it's quills will get finished and then . . . ?* Amma Pranaa thought she could take a stand against her parents and nearly met her death.

Now, this 'Ananse' story, whether it is sensible or not, take what you can from it and leave the rest in the air.

CHORUS: Eheeeeeeeeeeee . . .

Drumming and dancing for CHORUS *exit.*

CANTOR: [*Sings*]

Afei Anansesem yi yedereko	Now we are taking it away
Saa Anansesem yi yedereko	This our Ananse story.

CHORUS:

Anansesem yi yedereko oo	We are taking it away; this our Ananse story; we are taking it away.

CANTOR:

Anansesem a eye ma mmofra ne mpanyin yedereko	Our Ananse story which is for both young and old. We are taking it away.

CHORUS:

Anansesem yi yedereko oo	We are taking it away; this our Ananse story. We are taking it away.

They all go out as they have come in, taking everything away with them.
Bare stage. Solitary spot light on the Master Drummer.

MASTER DRUMMER:
Kron! Kron! Kron!!
The Drummer calls again;
What has the Master Drummer to say?
The Master Drummer says;
Condolence; condolence;
Accept my condolence.
For the cold night . . .
I wish you condolence;
For the thick darkness.
Sleep well; sleep well tonight;
Sleep well . . . like the python.

Blackout.

CURTAIN

The Firefly

A Play with traditional Drumming, Music and Dance

First published in *Yale Theatre*, Vol. 2 No. 2, 1969

First performed by the pupils of Anumle 'B' Middle Mixed School during 1973 Accra Schools Festival of Drama.

Cast

GIRL
BOY
OLD WOMAN
GIRL'S MOTHER
TWO MASKED FIGURES
PRIEST
TWO ATTENDANTS
CROWD

A corner in an African village kitchen. Nothing is seen except a coal pot. Beside it, an OLD WOMAN, *about eighty-five, sits on the floor. She wears rags.*

It is not cold during the day, but she is the type of old woman who needs fire around her at any time of the day.

A long, crooked walking stick lies on her right. Nearby is a silver pan, left unwashed from the previous day. Flies, cockroaches, and other such insects are the only friendly visitors to this place. To keep them off, the OLD WOMAN *smokes most of the time, leaving the stage overcast with smoke.*

She sits alone.

Enter a BOY *and a* GIRL, *both about seven years old. They halt a short distance from the* OLD WOMAN.

GIRL: Don't go any further!

BOY: I am not afraid of her.

GIRL: No, please; don't go to her! My mother tells me she eats children.

BOY: My father took me to the medicine man yesterday. I was given a talisman. Her evil spirit can't do anything to me.

GIRL: I can't come with you. I have no talisman.

BOY: [*Produces an amulet*] Come with me; I'll protect you.

GIRL: All right. [*Pause*] Mother said that light in the tree must be a firefly.

OLD WOMAN: [*In a singsong*] Little children . . . little children, come to me. I am so lonely.

BOY: Did you hear how her voice was shivering? She is under the spell of my talisman. I will ask her now!

GIRL: Please don't! I'm afraid.

BOY: [*He holds the amulet high and walks bravely to the* OLD WOMAN]. Old woman, this girl saw a big firefly behind her house yesterday. It flew away all over and sat on your roof. Where were you last night?

OLD WOMAN: In bed.

BOY: Yes, your body was in bed, but your soul, did it change into a firefly yesterday night?

OLD WOMAN: [*Enraged*] You! I will teach you to say such things to me! [*The* OLD WOMAN *tries to hit the* BOY *with her walking stick. She misses and, instead, the stick hits the* GIRL *on the temple.*] You little devil . . . You see . . . [*Soothes the* GIRL] Ohh . . . little darling . . . I am sorry. It wasn't you I meant to hit . . .

BOY: She will eat you!

GIRL: Ohhh . . . let me go! Let me go! Please don't eat me! Don't eat me! Let me go! [*Choked by smoke from the* OLD WOMAN'S *pipe, the* GIRL *starts coughing and sneezing. Enter her* MOTHER]

MOTHER: The gods protect you, my child!

GIRL: Mother . . . [*Coughs and sneezes*]

MOTHER: [*Lamenting*] Protect her, our most merciful guardian spirits. She is my last child.

GIRL: [*Runs to her* MOTHER] Mother, she'll eat me! [*Coughs and sneezes*]

MOTHER: Adjoa! . . . Adjoa! . . . What is wrong? Can you breathe well?

GIRL: [*Sneezes*] Ahh . . . Mother, I am dizzy!

MOTHER: Ahhh . . . the witch has caught my child! Great gods!

GIRL: Ahh . . . hold me, Mother. I am falling down. [*Sneezes*]

MOTHER: My child is murdered, my last child is . . .

GIRL: Ahh . . . Mother . . .

MOTHER: [*Beating the* OLD WOMAN] You witch . . . you red witch . . .

OLD WOMAN: You will kill me. You will . . .

MOTHER: What did you do to my daughter? What did you give her?

OLD WOMAN: It's tobacco . . . only tobacco . . .

MOTHER: You witch! Give me back my child! She is my last child. Give me back my child. [*To* BOY] What happened?

BOY: She called us here . . . and blew some smoke from her mouth into her face and . . .

OLD WOMAN: It is only tobacco from my pipe . . .

MOTHER: You liar. You've choked my daughter.

OLD WOMAN: No, it's . . .

MOTHER: Shut up! You have already eaten the souls of my four other children.

GIRL: [*Sneezes*] Ahh . . . Mother . . .

MOTHER: [*Lifts the* GIRL *onto her back*] Let's hurry to the medicine man. [*To the* OLD WOMAN] You won't eat my last child!

OLD WOMAN: [*Cursing*] May the gods reward you.

MOTHER: The words of a witch never go to the gods.

GIRL: Ahh . . . Mother . . .

MOTHER: You pray that my child should live. If she dies, I will come back here and skin you alive. [*To the* BOY] Don't stay here, she will eat you next. [*Exit* MOTHER *carrying* GIRL, *followed by* BOY]

OLD WOMAN: Oh . . . when . . . when . . . when will this torture finally come to an end? When will these dry bones find a resting place? [*A funeral dirge is heard*] My head is swimming . . . I see . . . [*Enter* TWO MASKED FIGURES, *another old woman and an old man*] I see . . . faces . . . faces . . . Ah, Mother . . . it is my mother . . . and father too . . . they've come . . . at last . . .

The dirge goes on. The OLD WOMAN *is deeply affected by the music. She begins humming to the funeral chant, with the* TWO MASKED FIGURES *forming a supporting chorus.*

FIGURES: I didn't know man's life is too short.
OLD WOMAN: Mother . . . I didn't know.
FIGURES: I didn't know man's life is too short.
OLD WOMAN: Father . . . I didn't know.
FIGURES: I didn't know man's life is too short.

Faster tempo.

OLD WOMAN: Mother . . . see . . .
FIGURES: I didn't know man's life is too short.
OLD WOMAN: Father . . . see . . .
FIGURES: I didn't know when it all began.
OLD WOMAN: It all began . . .
FIGURES: Tell it all to us.
OLD WOMAN: This is the story: [*Recitative*]
    I was very pretty once.
    My mother often said, 'Beauty is a curse.'
    My father warned me, 'Beauty is like the
    morning dew that dies with the first sun rise.'
    I thought they both envied me
    Until it was too late to learn.
FIGURES: I didn't know man's life is too short.
OLD WOMAN: I have more to tell . . .
FIGURES: Tell it all to us . . . We are all ears.
OLD WOMAN: [*Recitative*]
    My mother died and my father followed soon.
    My uncle would not have a spoiled child
    I was all for myself.
    Until the fruit began to sap.
FIGURES: I didn't know man's life is too short. I didn't know . . .
OLD WOMAN: There is still more to say.
FIGURES: Say it all . . . we are all ears.
OLD WOMAN: [*Recitative*] If you know where to find some rest . . . [*The*
    TWO MASKED FIGURES *turn their backs to the audience*] Please, take me
    to Mother. [*Exit* MASKED OLD WOMAN] Please, take me to Father.
    [*Exit* MASKED OLD MAN] I am tired, I need to rest. [*Drumming is
    heard in the distance. The* OLD WOMAN *is jerked back to herself*]
    Do I hear drumming?
    Or is the gong beating?
    Ohh . . . it is all my imagination
    The old should have illusions.
    Oh . . . I am hungry. I will roast some plantain for food. [*She
    rekindles the fire in the coal pot and begins roasting plantain. The whole
    stage is overcast with smoke from the coal pot*]
    Oh, man don't want me,
    And death refuse to take me.

My womb, my womb,
My crime is my womb.

Enter the village PRIEST, *followed by* FIRST ATTENDANT.

PRIEST: [*Surveys the room*] Attendant . . .

FIRST ATTENDANT: Yes, great one.

PRIEST: What do you see around you?

FIRST ATTENDANT: Thick smoke.

PRIEST: You have more yet to learn. These are the fumes let out by a witch when it is preparing to fly. As soon as it is dark, everything you see here will look like one big fire.

FIRST ATTENDANT: Wonders . . .

PRIEST: This room must be thoroughly cleansed. [*Noise of a* CROWD *is heard*]

FIRST ATTENDANT: The whole town must be on the way here.

PRIEST: Our detractors are going to pay highly for the lies they tell about us.

Enter SECOND ATTENDANT.

SECOND ATTENDANT: [*Kowtows*] Oh, most holy master . . . most invincible . . . most . . .

PRIEST: Yeeeesssss . . .

SECOND ATTENDANT: We've done as you commanded. The whole town is aroused and is on the way here.

PRIEST: Good. They will see enough to make them believe again that the gods are still powerful. [*Enter* A MAN] Send that man out! And don't allow anybody in here. This room is thickly under the spell of the very devil.

SECOND ATTENDANT: [*Kicking* THE MAN *out*] Out! Out of here! Do you want your spirit taken away from you?

PRIEST: The woman did a wise thing, she rushed the children to me. They wouldn't still be living. [*Drumming is heard from nearby. The* PRIEST *walks up and down, ringing his bell and waving his whisk. The drumming swells. The* PRIEST *dances much faster, whirling round several times. He sits. As in a trance*] Attendant, quick, impound the coal pot and the plantains. She has changed the child into plantain and is roasting it to eat. [*He goes to* OLD WOMAN *and slaps her*] You witch! You she-devil! What are you roasting?

OLD WOMAN: Some plantain. Only some plantain.

PRIEST: Why?

OLD WOMAN: Why?

PRIEST: Yes. Why are you roasting the plantain?

OLD WOMAN: To eat. I am hungry.

PRIEST: Ahh . . . you've confessed. You are hungry, eh? Hungry for child's meat! Right?

OLD WOMAN: No . . . not child's meat! I am hungry . . .

PRIEST: [*Slaps her*] You liar, you she-devil! This is child's meat.

OLD WOMAN: No . . . it is plantain.

PRIEST: It is child's meat changed into plantain. Confess it.

OLD WOMAN: Aooooooooooo . . .

PRIEST: Who was it you changed into the plantain?

OLD WOMAN: Nobody.

PRIEST: You liar! This plantain here is Adjoa, the child that was just rushed to my grove. Confess it! [*He slaps her*] Confess, foolish old woman.

OLD WOMAN: Aooooooooooooo . . . [*Falls heavily*]

PRIEST: Nobody should touch her . . . It is the god's work; they knocked her down. She lied to them. [*The* PRIEST *does a dance, circling the* OLD WOMAN *several times. As in a trance*] Ahhhh . . . horrible . . . horrible! Attendant, bring that silver pan over here. Hold it carefully; it is filled to the brim with blood.

FIRST ATTENDANT: [*Picking up the pan with care*] Who'd have believed this?

OLD WOMAN: Aooooooooooo . . . I will be dead.

FIRST ATTENDANT: You are free to die. I am not giving you back this blood.

PRIEST: Ahh . . . there are still more horrible revelations. [*Pan is brought to priest and after some incantations, drinks from empty pan*] Attendant, hold my left arm.

ATTENDANT: Yes, great one.

PRIEST: There now; I am transferring the blood I drank from the pan, through you back into the child. [*Incanting*] Flow . . . flow blood . . . flow back . . . flow . . . flow . . . flow . . . How do you feel now?

ATTENDANT: Wonders . . . wonders . . .

PRIEST: How?

ATTENDANT: Blood . . . blood . . .

PRIEST: Now I am going to transfer the blood from you into the child . . . stretch out your arm.

ATTENDANT: Yes, master.

PRIEST: Flow blood . . . flow . . . flow . . . flow . . .

ATTENDANT: Flow . . . flow . . . flow . . .

PRIEST: The child's got her blood perfectly replaced. She must be on the way back to normal by now. [*Pacing*] Attendant!

ATTENDANT: Master?

PRIEST: Are the drummers there?

ATTENDANT: Yes, master.

PRIEST: I don't hear them. Give them this. [*Throws down gold coin*]

ATTENDANT: [*Hides coin*] Music! Music! More music for the great master! [*Drumming comes out loud and heavy. Priest dances*]

PRIEST: [*Suddenly*] STOP! Stop the drumming!

ATTENDANT: Silence. Silence everybody.

PRIEST: [*Back in trance*] Ahhhh . . . ahhh . . . Quick, quick, impound the walking stick and the smoking pipe. She dazes people with the smoke from the pipe and kills them with the walking stick. [*Paces*] Attendant, the holy water . . . This room must be thoroughly cleansed. [*He is handed a bowl containing some dirty concoction. He sprinkles himself, then the Attendants*] I drive all evil spirits away . . . all evil forces away . . . all evil forces away . . . Hoot at all evil forces.

THE CROWD: Huuuuuuuuuuuuuu . . . huuuuuuuuuu . . . Huuuuuuuu . . . Evil spirits . . . Take your bad luck away with you.

PRIEST: I drive away all evil forces on my left. Hoot at it.

THE CROWD: Huuuuuuuu . . . Huuuuuuuu . . . Huuuuuuuu . . . all evil spirits on our left go away with your bad luck.

PRIEST: I drive away all evil forces on my right. Hoot at it.

THE CROWD: Huuuu . . . Huuuuuuuu . . . Huuuuuuuuu . . . all evil spirits on our right go far away with your bad luck. [*Drumming and dance*]

PRIEST: Attendant . . . Now, she must be made to confess all her sins.

FIRST ATTENDANT: I will give her the kola nuts.

PRIEST: You know your work.

FIRST ATTENDANT: I will give her the white kola nut first.

PRIEST: No . . . give her the red one. She is a hardened witch!

OLD WOMAN: [*Protesting*] No . . . No . . . No . . . The red one is poisoned . . . Oh . . . Crocodile bile! [*The kola nut is forced into her mouth*]

ATTENDANT: Eat it! Eat it!

PRIEST: Easy! Easy, Attendant. We don't believe in the use of force. Now confess about all the people you've killed since you started practising witchcraft.

OLD WOMAN: Ohhh . . . I'm dizzy . . . I'm dizzy!

PRIEST: That is the gods working. You must confess everything or you will never be forgiven.

OLD WOMAN: I didn't kill anybody.

PRIEST: That is no confession.

OLD WOMAN: Ohhh . . . I'm dying!

PRIEST: Yes, you will die, unless you tell the truth. Whose meat were you roasting on the fire?

OLD WOMAN: It was not meat . . . it was plant . . .

PRIEST: Lies! Lies, lies! You are an obstinate witch! You will die!

OLD WOMAN: No . . . I don't want to die.

ATTENDANT: Then tell the truth.

PRIEST: Was it the child's meat you were roasting on the fire?

OLD WOMAN: Ahhh . . . Ahhhh . . . help . . . help me . . . I don't want to die. I don't want to die.

PRIEST: It was the child's meat, wasn't it?

OLD WOMAN: No . . . Ahhh . . . yes, I am dying . . . ahhhhh . . .

PRIEST: [*Triumphantly*] Ah, she's confessed . . . she's confessed it was the child's meat she was roasting.

FIRST ATTENDANT: Poor child.

PRIEST: Now your pipe and your walking stick, what exactly are they for? Do you kill people with them?

OLD WOMAN: Ohhh . . . I don't want to die.

PRIEST: Do you club people to death with your walking stick?

OLD WOMAN: Yes . . . yes . . . help me . . . help me!

FIRST ATTENDANT: [*Down on his knees*] Oh, mighty one . . . you are truly the greatest.

PRIEST: What about the four boys who were killed by a falling tree? You pushed the tree on them, didn't you?

OLD WOMAN: Ahhh . . . ahhh . . . I am fainting . . . Yes . . .

PRIEST: You are the very embodiment of the devil.

FIRST ATTENDANT: She must not live; she will kill more people.

PRIEST: She will certainly not live, unless she comes out with all the names of the people she's killed.

OLD WOMAN: No . . . no . . . NOOOOOOOOOOOOO.

PRIEST: Yes . . . OUT WITH THEM! The storekeeper who died suddenly last month – you killed him, didn't you?

OLD WOMAN: Yes . . . yes . . . ah . . . ah . . . ah . . .

Enter A MAN.

FIRST ATTENDANT: Yes, I thought that man's death was too mysterious.

A MAN: My wife died of a snake bite about three months ago. Was it you who was the snake?

OLD WOMAN: Yes . . . yes . . . a . . . a . . . I . . . am . . . fain . . . ting.

MAN: I knew it. I knew it wasn't an ordinary snake.

The OLD WOMAN *collapses. Enter a* YOUNG MAN *and a* YOUNG WOMAN.

YOUNG MAN: My elder brother . . .

PRIEST: Don't touch her! She is unclean. Where are her relatives?

AN OLD MAN: [*Entering*] She has none. She was sent away from home when she was a young woman. [*Reflecting*] I still remember her very well. A beauty among the beauties, such was she . . . but she was too proud for a woman. She never married . . . and never had a child.

PRIEST: She ate all her children in her womb. A witch among the witches.

ANOTHER MAN: And she killed my wife . . . because we had five children in five years of our marriage.

PRIEST: Attendant, this unclean body must be sent to the grove, for cleansing. Then it shall be burned and the ashes destroyed. [*To* CROWD] Now, you may all go back to your homes and tell about the

great wonders that you have seen today. May the great gods guide
your footsteps. [*The* CROWD *disperses*]

OUNG MAN: [*To* YOUNG WOMAN] My elder brother died in a car
accident last year. She must have pushed the car into a ditch.

OUNG WOMAN: I am sure she did it.

CURTAIN

Lovenet
or
Just for the Fun of it

A Light Comedy

Characters

DR AMEGA ANNAN, *A family friend of Lawyer Frempong*
SISTER LEWA, *A friend to Mrs Frempong*
NURSE ADDO, *A catty nurse*
LAWYER FREMPONG, *A man-about-town*
MRS FREMPONG, *Wife of Lawyer Frempong*
ERIC NYARKO, *A medical student*
ABEREWA NTOMO, *A patient*
MR NTIFO, *A businessman – diamond smuggler – sometimes*
MRS NTIFO (FATI), *Wife of Mr Ntifo*
ALICE AYIM, *A teenage girl*

In a hospital where all the nations' sick and corrupted bodies get exposed.

A multiple set. Right of the set is Dr Annan's office and consulting room. The line is demarcated by a curtain that may be parted to reveal consulting room scene, and folded back, after the same. Left and downstage is the main acting area. For effect, characters trapped on stage all through the play, only a few entrances and exits are necessary.

NURSE ADDO *sits lazily behind a reception desk spraying disinfectant in the air. Enter* NTOMO, *an old woman of about seventy. She walks almost to stage centre. Stops. She has completely forgotten herself.*

ADDO: Maami[1] . . . [*Pause*] Hey, Maami!

NTOMO: Mmm . . .?

ADDO: Come this way.

NTOMO: Mmm?

ADDO: This way! Here! [*Whiff of disinfectant blows into* NTOMO's *face*]

NTOMO: Kyenku ee![2]

ADDO: I didn't mean to . . . here . . . let me wipe it with this.

NTOMO: Ahh . . . Wui! Wui! . . . Right in here . . . right in my eye.

ADDO: You're playing it up . . . Nothing got in there.

NTOMO: Pepper . . . pepper.

ADDO: [*Rubs*] Look . . . look. See? . . . nothing there.

NTOMO: Pain . . . pain.

ADDO: Open your eyes . . . slowly.

NTOMO: Ahhh . . . Ahhh.

ADDO: What is it again?

NTOMO: Pepper . . . hot pepper.

ADDO: Very infuriating. Nothing got into your eyes. Here! This way, sit here.

NTOMO: I won't!

ADDO: You will! Sit down!

NTOMO: Don't you see?

ADDO: See what?

NTOMO: My waist!

ADDO: What about your waist?

NTOMO: Locked up!

ADDO: [*Pushes* NTOMO *down with force*] I don't have the whole day.

---

[1] Maami = Woman.

[2] Kyenku ee = A venerable male god that abhors blood and corruption.

NTOMO: Kyenku ee!

ADDO: You should have a grandchild in the house.

NTOMO: Hmmm.

ADDO: Forget it.

NTOMO: I won't forget it! You children of today . . .

ADDO: Children of today . . . children of . . .

NTOMO: Don't interrupt me! You ostrich . . .

ADDO: Me?

NTOMO: You must be a very bad girl.

ADDO: A bad girl?

NTOMO: Yes, you look like one and have behaved like one to me.

ADDO: You dead brains get on my nerves. [*Pulls* NTOMO *roughly*] Sit here! This way!

NTOMO: Careful! You'll pull off my arm.

ADDO: Then it pulls off.

NTOMO: I won't say a word . . . not another word.

ADDO: Better. Now give me your particulars.

NTOMO: Particulars?

ADDO: Your name?

NTOMO: Name?

ADDO: God! Am I speaking to a piece of wood?

NTOMO: [*Slaps her*] No!

ADDO: What?

NTOMO: Enough is enough!

ADDO: You slapped me?

NTOMO: I did. And I enjoyed it very much. I allow people to push me around twice at a time . . . the third attempt . . . I do the pushing.

ADDO: Look here!

NTOMO: Again? I don't hesitate . . . I may be three times as old as you are, young woman, but I have slapped people twice as young as your age. Ask my granddaughter.

ADDO: It's alright.

NTOMO: It is not alright.

ADDO: It was only a little harmless shouting.

NTOMO: I gave you only a little harmless slap then.

ADDO: Settled then?

NTOMO: No! You are but a child. A child is a child, she listens. She does not shout a little harmless shouting at an old woman. In my days we listened to our elders and knew our place; that's why I've lived to this age.

ADDO: I only asked you to hurry up.

NTOMO: You shouted. You did not ask. You were shouting.

ADDO: I did not shout.

NTOMO: You did. And don't tell a lie! That's what that silly granddaughter of mine does in the house; tells a lie every minute.

I have an effective weapon for that kind of nonsense. Now, give me a chair!

ADDO: I'm sorry.

NTOMO: If you had any manners, you would have offered a chair to an old woman and stopped smashing my poor stiff waist on a hard bench.

ADDO: I am sorry. Please, sit down!

NTOMO: [*Sits*] Thank you. I talk too much. I know. But why shouldn't I talk? People want to turn this beautiful country into a second madhouse. Would have been better I had gone blind. The filth you people delight swimming in, my lips are too heavy to speak about it. Look at my granddaughter – sixteen years old, only sixteen years old and she thinks she's already a woman. Any tobacco?

ADDO: I don't smoke.

NTOMO: Don't. My granddaughter smokes even at her age. You should see that . . . like a baby monkey.

ADDO: May I have your particulars now?

NTOMO: No.

ADDO: Why?

NTOMO: I came to see a doctor . . . not you!

ADDO: I serve the doctor . . . And I shall need your particulars to help the doctor serve you.

NTOMO: I know that!

ADDO: May I have your particulars then? [*Begins to write*] Your name?

NTOMO: 'Aberewa'.

ADDO: Your real name, please.

NTOMO: That's what everybody calls me.

ADDO: 'Aberewa' means 'an old woman'.

NTOMO: Yes, I am an old woman.

ADDO: Did they call you 'Aberewa' when you were young?

NTOMO: No.

ADDO: What was your name when you were young?

NTOMO: Ntomo.

ADDO: What Ntomo?

NTOMO: Afua . . . Afua Ntomo.

ADDO: Thank you. [*Writes*] Afua Ntomo. How old are you?

NTOMO: Eh?

ADDO: Look here; don't waste my time!

NTOMO: To me? Speaking to me?

ADDO: I didn't mean any harm.

NTOMO: You shouted at me . . . you shouted. I can shout too, you know.

ADDO: Please don't shout.

NTOMO: I have forgiven you.

ADDO: Thank you. [*Pause*] Please, how old are you?

NTOMO: I was born not quite three festivals before 'Yaa Asantewa'[1] fought Sagranti.[2]

ADDO: Thank you.

NTOMO: Any more you want to know?

ADDO: What do you want to see the doctor about?

NTOMO: Everything. And old woman is always ill, you know.

ADDO: Yes . . . but what exactly is wrong with my kind grandmother?

NTOMO: My whole body. My head, my neck, my eyes, my ears and ah, yes, my WAIST! . . . 'Kooko'.[3]

ADDO: 'Maami' . . . don't you have any relative in the house to help you to the hospital?

NTOMO: Hmm . . . Awuran, I am glad you asked such a question. I have a granddaughter . . . sixteen years old but . . . well . . . her breasts have already popped up round and firm, would she stay in the house? No! She goes round after men her father's age.

Siren is heard louder and louder.

NTOMO: What is that noise?

ADDO: The siren . . . somebody is being rushed here. [SISTER LEWA *rushes in*]

LEWA: Nurse! Quick! Over here! Emergency!

ADDO: Yes, Sister.

LEWA: Get the emergency kit. Attempted suicide. [LEWA *rushes out*]

NTOMO: But where are you going? [ADDO *rushes out*] Oh, children of today. They like rushing about too much. It kills them.

Enter an intern, ERIC NYARKO. *He is a very handsome youth.*

NYARKO: [*Helping* NTOMO] Sit here please.

NTOMO: Are you the doctor?

NYARKO: I'm learning to be a doctor.

NTOMO: Tell me, what's all this rushing about? I was talking to the nurse, and suddenly she's vanished!

NYARKO: It's only a minor case.

NTOMO: Minor case? That's what I know about you doctors. When a case is minor, you rush. When it is as serious as mine you keep me on and on . . . waiting and waiting.

NYARKO: You relax, you'll be attended to . . . soon.

---

[1] An Asante Queenmother who led the Asante war against the British in 1900.
[2] Sagranti is Akan for Sir Garnant Wolsey, the British Commander in the War against the Asantes in 1897.
[3] Piles.

NTOMO: Thank you [*Irrelevantly*] You know, you are a very nice
young man.

NYARKO: Thank you.

NTOMO: And very handsome too.

NYARKO: Thank you.

NTOMO: I have a very pretty granddaughter. If she had not been such a
bad girl . . . I would have given her to you, free.

NYARKO: Thank you.

NTOMO: Are you going away too?

NYARKO: I have to help save that dying woman.

NTOMO: Dying woman? Okay, you may go. But when you see the doctor,
tell him Ntomo . . . 'Aberewa' Ntomo is waiting to see him. [*Enter
DOCTOR ANNAN*]

NYARKO: Hello, Doctor.

ANNAN: Eric . . . What's going on here?

NTOMO: Doctor.

ANNAN: Just a second . . . Just a second, old woman. [*Enter SISTER
LEWA*]

LEWA: Thank God you're here.

ANNAN: What's all the rushing about, Sister?

LEWA: Attempted suicide!

ANNAN: And who is that fool?

LEWA: She is not a fool, Doctor. [*Whispers*] Mrs Frempong!

ANNAN: Mrs Who?

LEWA: Frempong! The wife of Lawyer Frempong!

ANNAN: Jesus, my other soul! Hurry; let's hurry!

*Enter two orderlies carrying MRS FREMPONG on a stretcher, NURSE ADDO
reviving her.*

MRS FREMPONG: Ahh . . . ah . . . ah . . . let me die! Let me die!
[*MRS FREMPONG vomits*]

LEWA: Quick, take her inside!

MRS FREMPONG: Don't save me! I want to die! I want to die! [*Exit
orderlies with MRS FREMPONG*]

ANNAN: I shall need you, Sister, in there. And you Eric too. Nurse Addo . . .

ADDO: Sir.

ANNAN: Wipe up the vomit. [*Exit DOCTOR ANNAN, ERIC NYARKO and
SISTER LEWA*]

ADDO: [*Mops*] Kai . . .

NTOMO: I feel like vomiting. Where do I go to?

ADDO: Out there; outside! [*Exit NTOMO. ADDO mops floor. Enter NTIFO*]

NTIFO: Is she dead?

ADDO: Who?

NTIFO: The woman. Is she dead?

ADDO: Is she your wife?

NTIFO: I wish she were.

ADDO: Why do you want to know then?

NTIFO: She wanted to kill herself?

ADDO: Sir?

NTIFO: Yes.

ADDO: What can I do for you?

NTIFO: For me? Nothing . . . nothing, at all, I'm looking for . . . just looking for a strayed wife.

ADDO: And who is that strayed wife?

NTIFO: Fati, of course!

ADDO: Don't know her.

NTIFO: Don't know Fati? How long have you been working here?

ADDO: Is she here for treatment?

NTIFO: My wife ill? My wife will never be ill. She comes here for . . . for . . . for . . . How many new doctors have you here in this hospital?

ADDO: Two. Why?

NTIFO: That's all. Thank you very much. [*Exit* NTIFO. *He bumps into* NTOMO]

NTOMO: Watch where you're going.

NTIFO: Sorry, old woman. [*Exit* NTIFO]

NTOMO: Dirty money man. Doctor in now?

ADDO: Sit down.

NTOMO: Feel like vomiting again.

Enter DOCTOR ANNAN *and* ERIC NYARKO.

ADDO: Doctor is here.

NTOMO: Coming. [*Exits*]

NYARKO: That's a fast piece of good work, Doctor.

ANNAN: Only a minor case, Miss Addo.

ADDO: Yes, Doctor.

ANNAN: Mrs Frempong vomited again. Go in and wipe it up.

ADDO: Yes, Doctor.

ANNAN: And stay with her.

ADDO: Yes, Doctor.

Enter SISTER LEWA.

ANNAN: Sister, can I have a cup of coffee . . . I am in my office.

LEWA: Yes, Doctor. [*Exits*]

NYARKO: Doctor, may I ask you a question?

ANNAN: Students always ask questions. Go ahead.

NYARKO: How did you arrive at such a quick diagnosis? You looked like you knew your prescription even before you saw your patient.

ANNAN: I have treated the same cases over and over again. It's almost a national theatre; always about married people who cannot live

together but cannot separate. Broken hearted wives always drinking
poison but not quite enough of it to do them in. Rich married men
throwing money away on pretty young girls who want the money
but not the men. All the nation's mess and corruption finally find
their way into this little theatre. Are you married?

NYARKO: No, sir.

ANNAN: You are not likely to understand, then.

Enter SISTER LEWA.

LEWA: Want the coffee here, Doctor?

ANNAN: Sister, you must organize twenty-four-hour intensive
observation on your friend's wife. And make sure she receives the
most kindly attention from the nurses.

NYARKO: May I check up on something? [*Exit* NYARKO]

LEWA: Doctor, may I ask you something?

ANNAN: Women always ask questions. Go ahead.

LEWA: When are you men going to change for the better?

ANNAN: When women change for the best.

LEWA: Seriously. When is Lawyer Frempong changing this playboy life
of his? Ignoring a good woman like Mrs Frempong.

ANNAN: Don't get worried about Lawyer Frempong. Think about your
fourteen-year-old daughter.

LEWA: Doctor!

ANNAN: Yes.

LEWA: Look! Over there!

ANNAN: Good God!

LEWA: Lawyer Frempong and his latest toadfish! I feel like scratching
that man's eyes out of their thick sockets! What . . .

ANNAN: Leave him to me . . . And don't say a word to him about
his wife.

LEWA: How can I keep quiet over . . .?

ANNAN: Not a word from you. Promise?

LEWA: If you say so.

Enter LAWYER FREMPONG *and* ALICE AYIM.

LAWYER: Hello, Sister . . . I didn't know you were on duty?

LEWA: I am on duty.

LAWYER: Good . . . good . . . beautiful . . . Doctor, how are you?

ANNAN: Fine.

LAWYER: You all meet a very nice lady. Alice, meet the greatest, the
sweetest and the most skilful doctor. No bragging and no boasting,
lady. You are standing in front of the best doctor this country,
Africa, and the whole world has produced together since the fall of
Timbuctu. The pride of medical science, the doctor's doctor and

above all a gentleman who has only one wife and swears not to make
a pass at another woman. The one and only doctor.

ANNAN: Hello, young woman.

ALICE: Sir.

LEWA: Hello.

ALICE: Hello.

LAWYER: Can I see you alone, Doctor? In private!

ANNAN: I know your problem. You want another effective
contraceptive.

LAWYER: No . . . no, not that this time. Almost round about case . . .
similar but not familiar . . . Can I see you now . . . in private?

ANNAN: You are seeing me now.

LAWYER: No . . . no . . . no. In private. Please.

ANNAN: Fine. But don't take too much of my time.

LAWYER: Thirty seconds, no more. In your office then.

ANNAN: You know what to do, Sister. Excuse me!

LEWA: Lawyer.

LAWYER: Yes, dear?

LEWA: How is Mrs Frempong?

LAWYER: Fat and fighting fit.

ALICE: [Guffaws] Excuse me. [Silence. All eyes on ALICE] Why are you all
looking at me like that for? Why? Why?

LEWA: How old are you? [ALICE *does not answer; instead, she nervously opens
her bag, pulls out a piece of chewing gum, puts it in her mouth and begins
munching noisely*]

ANNAN: Excuse me. [*Exits*]

LAWYER: Excuse me ladies. [*Exits*].

LEWA: Calm your nerves and take a chair.

ALICE: I won't sit!

LEWA: Well, keep standing.

ALICE: I won't stand anywhere!

LEWA: Excuse me then. [*Exit* LEWA]

ALICE *nervously tapping her shoes on the floor. She finally slumps into chair and as
she begins mopping sweat from her brow, the screen to* DR ANNAN'S *office
parts, revealing* DR ANNAN *and* LAWYER FREMPONG.

ANNAN: Well?

LAWYER: Troubles, Doctor, are tricky situations and tricky situations
can turn even tarts into adorable nymphs. Look . . . look at me; an
old man of my age bathed in goose pimples and sweating on a cold
morning. And all because of that little tricky sneak out there. It's
no laughing matter; seriously, that tart out there, that trollope, the
little lick-penny's got me in deep trouble . . . right up to here in mud
. . . no, quicksand.

ANNAN: How?

LAWYER: She's pregnant.

ANNAN: Pregnant?

LAWYER: That's what she tells me. The slut!

ANNAN: Well?

LAWYER: She rushed to my office this morning. Held me up . . . shirt, tie and all, like this! [ANNAN *laughs*] Don't laugh, friend. It isn't funny at all.

ANNAN: But what does she want?

LAWYER: Money! What else? She wants one hundred cedis. One good hundred cedis.

ANNAN: What for?

LAWYER: Abortion. What else?

ANNAN: Give her the money.

LAWYER: At this time of the month?

ANNAN: Well . . . so?

LAWYER: Please, help me.

ANNAN: How?

LAWYER: Look, she complained about a little headache. I convinced her to come to you. When she comes, give her some medicine, something strong, that will drop the thing in one second!

ANNAN: Can't do that.

LAWYER: For old time's sake. See, I have six children already.

ANNAN: Sorry.

LAWYER: I will kiss your feet if you want me to do that. I have six children . . . all girls . . . and the expenses. Six children . . . all in school . . . and that little thing is trying to rob my pocket of a hundred good cedis. I begged her, even went down on my two knees . . . look at all that; an old man of my age kissing the feet of a girl my daughter's age. She should give me a little time; just more time to pay my children's school fees. That's all a good Christian can ask of a little virgin; but you must see the sneak. I was down on my knees like this . . . then, she held my tie up this way . . . pulled me up . . . pulled me down this way. And all the time shouting and cursing and crying . . . very embarrassing. But what can a man of my status do in a situation like this?

Knock. NTIFO *zooms in without waiting for an answer.*

NTIFO: Morning, Doctor.

ANNAN: Hello, Mr Diamond. Long time no see. What brings you here today?

NTIFO: Where do I sit?

ANNAN: What can I do for you?

NTIFO: I am fat. I must sit.

ANNAN: There.

NTIFO: Good. [*Coughs*]

LAWYER: Can I get up now?

ANNAN: Please do. I think I have finished with you.

LAWYER: You haven't even started with me.

ANNAN: Give me a second . . . just a second . . . What can I do for you, Mr Diamond?

NTIFO: I want to talk to you.

ANNAN: Go ahead.

NTIFO: A very serious case.

ANNAN: I'm listening.

NTIFO: And very personal.

ANNAN: I'm still listening.

NTIFO: I came to see you . . . No, send him out first. I am a businessman, I must protect my personal integrity.

LAWYER: I am a lawyer, I champion and defend businessmen.

NTIFO: I want to discuss a very serious thing with the doctor, if you don't mind.

LAWYER: I am discussing a very, very serious case.

NTIFO: Mine is more serious than yours.

LAWYER: Mine is very serious.

NTIFO: Mine is between life and death.

LAWYER: Mine is death.

NTIFO: Then die in peace! I can bury a hundred of your kind!

ANNAN: Just a second.

NTIFO: Send him out!

ANNAN: Wait!

NTIFO: He should do the waiting, but outside . . .

ANNAN: Excuse us then, Mr Frempong.

LAWYER: But my case?

ANNAN: In a moment.

LAWYER: But I came first.

ANNAN: Come back later.

LAWYER: You have not finished with me. My case is still pending.

ANNAN: You have no case.

LAWYER: No case? With all the sweat . . . And that little virgin darling out there waiting to defraud an innocent old man? Please, Doctor, consider my case . . . my status . . . my reputation . . . integrity.

ANNAN: I shall consider everything. But come back later.

LAWYER: This is unjust.

NTIFO: I am a businessman, and I care about what works for me, not for what is 'just or unjust' . . . or . . .

ANNAN: Just excuse us a second, Lawyer, please.

LAWYER: Where is this country going to when any criminal with enough stolen money is respectable? Okay . . . I am waiting . . . waiting for you outside. [*Exit* LAWYER]

NTIFO: I can sue him for slander . . . defamation . . . defamation of character.

ANNAN: He is a lawyer.

NTIFO: I am merciful. Now to my case. I came to report a very serious case.

ANNAN: Let's hear you.

NTIFO: Doctor, I came to report one case . . . but right out there I have just met a second serious case. More serious than the first.

ANNAN: Let's hear you.

NTIFO: My wife has been visiting your hospital for the past five years.

ANNAN: I know.

NTIFO: Your treatment has not worked so far; we still have no child. Now I know the problem.

ANNAN: You do?

NTIFO: Clear as daylight and as sure as sand. My wife has been mixing blood. She has another lover, here, in this hospital.

ANNAN: This is serious.

NTIFO: Very, very serious. I am a very hard man. Warn all your young doctors. Powerful jujus are my best friends, so warn all your young doctors. If I catch anyone playing with my wife, I'll 'die' him. Fast.

ANNAN: I'll warn them all.

NTIFO: Case one closed. Case number two. You know, I have all the money in the world but no child. My wife has given me no child. But I am lucky.

ANNAN: Lucky?

NTIFO: Lucky. I have a girl friend.

ANNAN: I see.

NTIFO: And I am blessed!

ANNAN: Blessed?

NTIFO: She is pregnant.

ANNAN: Your wife?

NTIFO: My girl friend.

ANNAN: Very happy news indeed.

NTIFO: Let me finish. My girl friend is pregnant. And I am ready to pay all the money in the world [*Pulls out wads of money*] . . . all the money in the world. I must have that child! But that girl! That silly girl!

ANNAN: Yes?

NTIFO: She doesn't want the child! Silly! Silly!

ANNAN: What does she want?

NTIFO: Abortion, of course . . . and . . . immediate! I have done everything to convince her to let the pregnancy stay but you want to see that foolish girl! Running here, running there, knocking beer bottles about here, smashing drinking glasses there, she even insulted me; fancy that, a man of my stomach and status. Finally she held my suit and tore off one pocket completely! She was wild! Very wild.

I swear I have never, in all the fifty-five years of my life, seen a girl that wild. And she is expecting a baby, my baby too . . . very childish of her, isn't it?

ANNAN: What does she want?

NTIFO: Two hundred cedis.

ANNAN: You have the money.

NTIFO: No . . . no . . . no . . . you don't get the picture. She wants the money to help destroy my baby. She wants to kill my only baby!

ANNAN: And you want my help?

NTIFO: Very much. Very, very much.

ANNAN: Relax now. What do you think I can do to help you?

NTIFO: One thing. I came down tracking my strayed wife and fell into my girl friend here. She is right out there. Tells me she's come to see you. I'm sure it's all about her abortion case. Please help me; I want the child, badly.

ANNAN: How? If I send her away she'll go to another doctor.

NTIFO: Don't send her away. Keep her here. And give her some strong medicine, something very, very strong that will make the pregnancy stick strong . . . very, very strong. [*Knock.* NTOMO *peeps in*]

NTOMO: May I come in now?

NTIFO: You can't come in.

ANNAN: Come in.

NTIFO: I protest . . . I have a case . . . a very serious case.

ANNAN: Please sit down, old woman.

NTOMO: Thank you.

ANNAN: Bring the girl friend in later, Mr Diamond.

NTIFO: No . . . no . . . I'll bring her in now. Right now . . . Right this minute. [*Exits*]

ANNAN: What can I do for you, old woman?

NTOMO: Many things. My head, my neck, my eyes . . . By the way, have you seen a young girl . . . about sixteen . . . somewhere in here?

ANNAN: No. Why?

NTOMO: Somebody much like my granddaughter flashed past my dim eyes but . . .

ANNAN: Maybe your eyes.

NTOMO: Ahh, yes, yes, my eyes and neck and my head too and . . . Yes . . . my waist.

ANNAN: Please sit down and relax . . . relax.

NTOMO: I am relaxed!

ANNAN: Breathe in . . . in . . .

Screen shuts off as scene shifts back to reception area.

LAWYER: This is a hospital . . . a public place . . . please, don't ask me to go down on my knees.

ALICE: My money.

LAWYER: Don't create another scene, we are in public.

ALICE: I know where we are. I want my money.

LAWYER: I have to go to the bank.

ALICE: You were going to go to the bank on Monday. You just missed going to the bank on Tuesday. You misplaced your cheque book on Wednesday. You went to the court all day yesterday. Today, Friday . . .

LAWYER: One hundred good cedis? Alice . . . be a bit reasonable.

ALICE: Are you giving me the money? [*Enter* ERIC NYARKO *from ward*] Eric!

NYARKO: Alice! What are you doing here?

ALICE: I thought you said you were off duty today.

NYARKO: I'm meeting a patient. What time is it?

LAWYER: Ten o'clock.

ALICE: Oh . . . meet Mr Frempong.

NYARKO: Mr Frempong?

LAWYER: The same.

NYARKO: I'm just from the ward. Doctor Annan may want to see you.

LAWYER: I have seen him.

NYARKO *pulls* ALICE *aside*.

NYARKO: Alice, do you know that man?

ALICE: Mr Frempong?

NYARKO: Yes.

ALICE: I know him.

NYARKO: I know you know him. But what is he to you?

ALICE: Oh Eric, don't ask such a silly question! You know I know people.

NYARKO: Eh?

ALICE: He's a friend to my girl friend. [*Enter* NTIFO *from* DR ANNAN'S *office*]

ALICE: Oh, Mr Diamond, you're here. Did you see the doctor?

NTIFO: Yes. And he wants to see you. Now!

ALICE: What for?

NTIFO: [*Roughly pulling* ALICE] No questions!

NYARKO: Look here . . .

NTIFO: Nothing of that from you, young man. Let's go, my girl!

LAWYER: Where are you taking the lady?

NTIFO: Why do you want to know? Is she your daughter?

LAWYER: And is she your daughter?

ALICE: Leave me alone.

NYARKO: Wait a minute!

NTIFO: Why? Is she your sister?

NYARKO: I was talking to her.

NTIFO: The doctor wants to talk to her too. Let's go, my girl!

LAWYER: I was talking to her.

NTIFO: Don't listen to any of them, my girl. Let's go!

LAWYER: This is the second time this morning that . . . that . . . who are you by the way?

NYARKO: Yes, who are you?

NTIFO: Who are you two nosy people?

NYARKO: Who are you too?

LAWYER: Who are you too?

NTIFO: [*To* ALICE] My girl, who are these people?

LAWYER: I am a lawyer.

NTIFO: I am a businessman. [*Pulls* ALICE] Let's go now. The doctor is waiting!

NYARKO: Wait!

NTIFO: What again?

NYARKO: Alice . . . Do you know this strange man? What is he to you?

ALICE: Eric, Eric. But you know I know people.

NYARKO: I know 'you know people' but what is he to you?

NTIFO: You don't know? She is my girl, very serious girl friend.

LAWYER: Impossible. She is my girl friend.

NTIFO: No, she is mine.

LAWYER: She is mine . . . I drove her here!

NTIFO: Ask her; she was in my house only yesterday.

LAWYER: She is my serious girl friend; ask her too.

NYARKO: Stop, you two!

NTIFO: Why should I? She is my girl . . . I have every right . . .

LAWYER: She is mine.

NTIFO: She is mine.

LAWYER: She is mine.

NTIFO: Mine.

LAWYER: Mine.

NYARKO: Stop that, you two!

LAWYER: Don't interfere.

NYARKO: Why shouldn't I?

NTIFO: Why should you? Is she your sister?

NYARKO: She is my girl friend.

NTIFO: Impossible. I saw her only last night.

LAWYER: She's been with me all this morning.

NYARKO: Keep quiet, you all! Alice, which of all the men here is your boy friend?

ALICE: You, Eric.

LAWYER: What?

NTIFO: You must be ill. Come, let's go to the doctor. [*Pulls* ALICE *roughly*]

ALICE: Let go of me!

NTIFO: What! You? A woman talk to me like that?

ALICE: You can go hang yourself.

NTIFO: No. I won't hang myself. I want to live! I want to live and father our baby. Or aren't you pregnant, by me?

LAWYER: Pregnant? By you? No, she is pregnant, but by me.

NTIFO: No, she is pregnant by me!

LAWYER: She said she was pregnant by me!

NTIFO: No, by me!

LAWYER: No, by me!

NTIFO: No, by me!

LAWYER: I am responsible. Ask her.

NTIFO: I am responsible. Ask her.

NYARKO: But is she pregnant? Alice, are you pregnant?

ALICE: No, Eric; I'm not pregnant.

NTIFO: WHAT?

LAWYER: WHAT? But you wanted one hundred cedis this morning to . . . to . . .

NTIFO: She took two hundred from me last night.

NYARKO: Alice, did you take two hundred cedis from that man?

ALICE: No, Eric.

NTIFO: You did.

ALICE: Prove it!

LAWYER: Yes . . . prove it!

NTIFO: I don't know law; I know the truth . . . and I know two hundred cedis . . .

NYARKO: Alice . . . Alice . . . and I thought you were so pure.

ALICE: Eric, please . . . please . . . just . . . just for the fun of it . . . There's no love, no love . . .

NYARKO: And I thought you so . . . so innocent.

NTOMO *approaches.*

NTOMO: Is that not my granddaughter Yaa? Yaa? Yaa Ayim.

ALICE: [*Rushes to* LAWYER] Take me away, take me away from here?

NTIFO: Don't go to him. Come to me.

ALICE: Take your hands off me!

LAWYER: Please, leave her alone.

NTIFO: You leave her alone.

LAWYER: She doesn't want you.

NTIFO: She doesn't want you either.

NYARKO: Oh . . . Alice . . . Alice . . . I trusted you so much . . . so much!

NTOMO: Yaa, what are you doing there between two old men? Hey . . . I'm talking to you! What are you doing here between two men? [*Slaps her*]

ALICE: God!

NTOMO: [*Insulting*] Effoww . . . Have you swept your room this morning?

LAWYER: Old woman, don't be too severe on a lady like . . .

NTOMO: Who are you? Who are you two men?

LAWYER: I am a lawyer.

NTOMO: [*To* NTIFO] You too, who are you?

ALICE: Leave them alone! Leave them alone!

NTOMO: Yiee? Talking to me like that! You talking to me like that! [*Removes one sandal*] Open your mouth again and . . .

ALICE: Please . . . Please . . . help me! Help! She'll hit me.

NTOMO: Talk like that again and I'll mess your face up quick.

LAWYER: Enough! Enough! One doesn't go about freely messing up other people's faces these days.

NTOMO: A fine world you are making of your life.

NYARKO: Nana . . . enough . . . forgive her . . . she begs . . .

NTOMO: She is a bad girl. You look at her . . . look at something. And what is that paint you have on your mouth? And that dress too . . . all the way here. You want to show all your nakedness to the public? Go ahead, show everything in public. Let me go home now.

NYARKO: Let me help you with your sandals.

NTOMO: Thank you. In my days, young man, women dressed up from the nape to the toe. In those days when you wanted even a prostitute, you had to pay one red pound. But look . . . look at the way she's dressed up there? Who will pay two shillings for that?

NYARKO: I will see you off at the gate.

NTOMO: Don't worry; I'll see myself off. Hey, Yaa, I'm going home! I expect you there by the time I get to the house. Standing there all painted up like a woman, have you swept your room today? [*Exit* NTOMO]

NTIFO: Hey, Alice, don't leave yet! I want my two hundred cedis back! Now!

LAWYER: What two hundred cedis?

NTIFO: I wasn't talking to you.

LAWYER: I am talking to you.

NTIFO: Don't come into this.

LAWYER: I will come into this. Did she force you to give her any money?

NTIFO: Yes.

LAWYER: Prove it!

NTIFO: I don't know law. But I know when I have been swindled. [*To* ALICE] My money! Quick!

ALICE: Eric . . . help me.

NYARKO: How?

ALICE: He will kill me!

NYARKO: Mr . . .

NTIFO: Diamond.

NYARKO: Mr Diamond, leave the young lady to me.

NTIFO: Pay me back my money and . . .

NYARKO: You leave her to me.

NTIFO: You pay me back my money and I'll give her all to you.

NYARKO: I'll talk to her. Alone, first.

NTIFO: Na money na hand; na woman na free . . .

NYARKO: I want to be sure.

NTIFO: Guarantee . . .

NYARKO: Somebody is bringing me money here in a few minutes. You'll have all your money before you leave the hospital.

NTIFO: I'll wait, I'm waiting here.

NYARKO: Wait here. Come with me Alice. [NYARKO *pulls* ALICE *away from* MR FREMPONG *and* NTIFO. *As two men begin to argue hotly further upstage,* NYARKO *confronts* ALICE, *downstage*] I'm going to pay back whatever you owe that man. That's the last good service I can offer you. After that, it is all over between us. I don't know you any more and I don't want to know anything or remember or even think about you again . . . ever!

ALICE: Eric, let me explain.

NYARKO: Explain? I have seen everything myself.

ALICE: I love you.

NYARKO: Ha!

ALICE: Honest.

NYARKO: Thank you very much.

ALICE: I'm on my knees.

NYARKO: Rot there.

ALICE: Please, Eric, you must understand. I was unhappy in the house. My grandmother, she kept nagging . . . nagging . . . all the time . . . and you have no time for me . . . always with your books.

NYARKO: So you should swindle and trade yourself to old men?

ALICE: And money . . . money tempted me.

NYARKO: When I was struggling, studying and suffering, all for the sake of our future, you were jumping about . . . swinging and swindling and making yourself popular . . . No more! It's all over . . . all over . . . between . . .

ALICE: [*On her knees*] Please.

NYARKO: I don't want to hear anything.

ALICE: Eric!

NYARKO: I don't know you . . . any more.

ALICE: Eric, wait!

NYARKO: I have nothing! [NYARKO *rushes out.* ALICE *chases after him.* NYARKO *bumps into* MRS NTIFO *who is entering.* MRS NTIFO'S *bag falls.*] Sorry.

FATI: [*Picks up bag*] Never mind. Here is the money. [*Gives bag to* NYARKO] I think my husband's been shadowing me. I must be off.

NTIFO: [*From a distance*] Hey . . . hey . . . Fati . . . don't run away.

FATI: God help me.

NTIFO: Stay there! Today, you are caught, red-handed!

FATI: Have I stolen anything of yours?

ALICE: Eric, who is this woman?

NYARKO: You can't ask me that question.

ALICE: [*Grabs him by the belt*] Don't play that with me. Who is that . . .?

NYARKO: Easy . . . easy, Alice.

ALICE: Make your answer quick and fast. Or I'll . . .

FATI: Leave Eric alone, young girl . . .

NTIFO: In front of me . . . your husband?

ALICE: Who is she?

NYARKO: She is Fati.

ALICE: I know she is Fati. Now, what is she to you?

NYARKO: I know her . . .

ALICE: I know you know her. How?

NYARKO: In the same way as these two men.

ALICE: Eric, I'm serious! Who is this woman?

NYARKO: You getting jealous? What, of me?

ALICE: Look here . . . don't make my blood start boiling. What is she to you?

NYARKO: Relax . . . relax . . . she only brought me money! The money I am going to use to pay your two hundred cedis debt.

NTIFO: Fati, what are you doing here?

FATI: What are you doing here yourself?

NTIFO: You must be ashamed of yourself! A married and an elderly woman chasing after small . . . small boys.

FATI: What of you . . . what about your small . . . small girls?

NTIFO: [*To* NYARKO] Look here! What are you doing there holding my travelling bag?

LAWYER: Things are getting too complicated. Alice, I brought you here, let me take you home.

ALICE: I'm not leaving here for all the money in the world! I'm staying here until I know what Eric is to that old woman.

FATI: Watch your mouth, small girl . . . who is an old woman?

NTIFO: Never mind about your age. What is this young man to you?

FATI: What is this young girl to you?

ALICE: Eric, what is this old woman to you?

NYARKO: Ask her.

ALICE: Hey . . . who are you? And what is Eric to you?

NTIFO: That's my question too.

FATI: You can't ask me that.

LAWYER: Can I come in?

NTIFO: You can't come in. My wife should tell me what my precious travelling bag is doing with HIM!

ALICE: [*Snatches bag from* NYARKO] What's in that bag? Let's see . . . [ALICE *pulls out two beautiful shirts*] Oh, I see . . . so that's how you get your beautiful shirts? [*Pushes shirts into his hand*] Here! Take your shirts back!

NTIFO: [*Snatches bag from* ALICE] Give me back my bag. [*Looks into bag*] What? Plenty of money, so? My money! And all that for him? Young man, you've killed me! Why? So I have all the time been smuggling diamonds and making money to pay you! You killed me.

LAWYER: [*Pointing to* ALICE] She killed me too.

NTIFO: Fati, I gave you all the money in the world to make you happy. Why did you do this to me?

FATI: But I wasn't seeing you. How can a woman stay alone one year with all the money but not her man?

NTIFO: So you paid him money . . . my money, to do just that for you?

FATI: Were you not paying her to do just that, too? Or you think I didn't know what's been going on between you and that . . .?

ALICE: Don't point your finger at me!

FATI: I will point my finger where I like.

ALICE: But don't you dare come to Eric again! You hear? If I catch you with him again, you'll see what I'm really made of.

FATI: And you at all, why are you so officious about Eric? Are you his sister?

ALICE: I am his fiancée.

FATI: His what?

ALICE: His girl friend!

FATI: What? [*Snatches shirts from* NYARKO] Give me back my shirts. You lie-lie man!

NTIFO: You lie-lie woman!

FATI: You lied to me! You told me you had no girl friend.

NYARKO: You never told me about your husband.

NTIFO: She never told you about me?

FATI: Why should I? Were you ever in the house?

NTIFO: Why should I? Have you ever given me any peace in the house?

FATI: Why should I? Have you stopped following small girls?

NTIFO: Have you stopped following small boys?

LAWYER: Young man . . . you've done wrong. Something unpardonable and legally wrong.

NYARKO: And you have done something morally right!

LAWYER: It is alright for a married man to go following an unmarried woman . . . but for you to follow a lawfully married woman is something far outside accepted decency and the law of the land.

FATI: But if the married woman is left all alone in the house and she is hungry . . . what is she supposed to do?

LAWYER: You still have no right to share another man's bed.

ALICE: Eric, I'm ashamed of you . . . an old woman like that?

NYARKO: I am also ashamed of you . . . old men like them?

LAWYER: I think we have seen enough for one morning. Shall I take you home, young woman?

NYARKO: You are not taking her anywhere!

LAWYER: Calm down, young man. I know she is your girl friend! But she allowed me to bring her here.

NYARKO: You brought her here! You find pleasure in wasting money and time on girls your daughter's age! Do you know where your wife is right this minute?

LAWYER: Eh? You are not telling me . . . you don't mean my wife is here flirting with one of the doctors?

FATI: What if she is?

LAWYER: Stop that! This is no joking matter.

NTIFO: You have been following other girls.

LAWYER: But not other people's wives.

NYARKO: Don't know if the married women are any different from those hot harlots.

FATI: Who is a harlot?

ALICE: You.

FATI: What of you?

ALICE: Am I married?

FATI: What is marriage when you can't see your husband?

NTIFO: You fooled me . . . you all fooled me.

LAWYER: Nobody fools with my wife! Nobody, you hear me? She is my wife! Lawfully married wife with children. Look here, young man, she is my legal wife. Nobody plays with my wife. Nobody touches my wife . . . Nobody!

ALICE: Why rage and shout! You told me you never loved your wife.

LAWYER: Never!

ALICE: You did! You promised you were going to divorce her last week.

LAWYER: Never!

ALICE: You lie!

LAWYER: Prove it.

ALICE: You know you promised me . . . you know you did.

LAWYER: I never promised you anything! I never promise!

ALICE: You monster! You . . .

NYARKO: Alice, don't.

ALICE: He is a dangerous man.

NYARKO: Dangerous? What of you?

NTIFO: And what of you . . .?

FATI: Are you any different?

LAWYER: You are all sick! Sick! Sick!

NYARKO: What of you?

LAWYER: I am not a fool!

Enter NURSE ADDO *from ward.*

ADDO: Please help me restrain Mrs Frempong.

LAWYER: Mrs Who?

ADDO: Mrs Frempong, your wife. She just woke up and is trying to come
down here to see you.

LAWYER: My wife? Here?

ADDO: Don't you know?

LAWYER: What is she doing here?

NYARKO: Trying to recover from the poison you forced on her.

LAWYER: Forced? Araba? Attempted suicide? When?

NYARKO: When you were out following small girls.

LAWYER: No more of that. [*Enter* MRS FREMPONG, *supported by* SISTER
LEWA]

LEWA: This is not my fault, Mr Frempong. She's heard of her rival and
wants to see her.

LAWYER: My dear, Araba, but . . . what happened?

MRS FREMPONG: Where is my rival? Where is the woman who can love
so well that you want to sacrifice me, Araba, and your six children
all for her . . . where is she?

LAWYER: Not now . . . not now, darling . . . let me take you home.

Enter DR ANNAN.

ANNAN: What are you doing here? You should be nursing Mrs Frempong.

LEWA: I tried, Doctor, she won't stay in bed; she insisted on seeing her
husband.

MRS FREMPONG: I heard that my husband, even on my death bed, is
here, with my rival, to mock me. I must see that woman; I must see
the woman who could turn my husband's mind against me, his wife,
his home, and his six children.

LAWYER: Don't talk like that, Araba.

MRS FREMPONG: I'm dying, my husband, tell that woman . . . that
wonderful woman, she must take good care of you . . . of you . . .
and the children. [*Collapses*]

ANNAN: Take her inside.

LAWYER: God! God! God!

ANNAN: Don't swear at me! Go home . . . you all go home. You're all
sick . . . sick . . . but no hospital . . . no doctor can cure you . . . go
home! [*Exit* DOCTOR, MRS FREMPONG *and* NURSES]

NYARKO: You are the one I blame for this.

ALICE: Oh yes, you didn't go following somebody's wife.

NTIFO: Young woman, now that I know you are not pregnant, may I
have my money back . . . or young man, you said you're paying me.

NYARKO: I don't owe you a pesewa.

NTIFO: Okay! Young woman, my money.

ALICE: Did I ask you to give me any money?

NYARKO: Nothing of that; you're paying back his two hundred cedis.

ALICE: The money I gave you yesterday. That's part of it.

FATI: [*To* NYARKO] You have to pay me back.

NYARKO: What for?

FATI: For the money I lavished on you . . . and the beautiful shirts . . .

NYARKO: My shirts too . . .

FATI: Yes. The shirt you're wearing now. I bought it for you. And I want it back, now!

NYARKO: Here?

FATI: Here! I want to expose your bony chest . . .

NYARKO: In public?

FATI: What of it? Quick! My shirt!

ALICE: Stop that! Stop that, you fool!

FATI: Why should I?

NTIFO: Yes, why should she stop? Go ahead, wife. I'll give you a hand if you like.

LAWYER: Stop that, you all.

NTIFO: Why should I? A fellow man with the same rod as I have has been feeding fat on me. I struggled, through fire, smuggled diamonds all the year, and there he was, dressing up in fashion from my dirty money.

LAWYER: A wife is always a wife. When all is said and concluded, a man always goes back home to his legal wife. I am going back to my wife. You may stay here and fight over what is already lost and defend a girl that has never been yours.

NTIFO: But my two hundred cedis.

FATI: What two hundred cedis?

NTIFO: This has nothing to do with you.

FATI: You have all your money in there.

NTIFO: Not that . . . Your 'part-timer' owes me two hundred cedis.

FATI: You do? How?

NYARKO: Ask her.

FATI: I'm asking you.

ALICE: Don't ask him, ask me.

NTIFO: I don't care who asks who. I want my money. Two hundred solid.

FATI: How did you come to owe my husband two hundred cedis?

NYARKO: Ask her.

FATI: You gave that small girl two hundred cedis? What for?

NTIFO: Not your business.

FATI: I am your wife! Tell me how she came to owe you that much money and I'll make her cough it out. Hey, young woman, the two hundred cedis . . .

ALICE: Do I owe you any money?

FATI: Nothing like that! You can share my husband's bed with me but you can't interfere with his money. Our two hundred cedis now or . . .

Enter NTOMO.

NTOMO: Enough! Enough! You all!

ALICE: Grandmother!

NTOMO: You thought I left . . . I have been out back there looking at you all making bigger fools of yourselves.

ALICE: Grandmother!

NTOMO: Haven't you so-called modern people made fools of yourselves long enough?

ALICE: Old Grandmother. Thank God you came.

NTOMO: I know you always need your grand past to save you. After messing yourself up so long, you now know you have a past to fall back on. Lucky for you I was not blinded. Come with me; you should thank your stars I was not blinded this morning. Follow me now. I'll take you home. [*Exit* NTOMO *with* ALICE]

NYARKO: God. I'm in the wrong world.

FATI: You?

NTIFO: You?

Blackout.

CURTAIN